unFINISHED
BUSINESS

AN ASSISTANT COACH'S PERSPECTIVE ON THE DRIVE FOR THE NATIONAL CHAMPIONSHIP

Ron Brown

ExHUSKER PRESS
A DIVISION OF CROSS TRAINING PUBLISHING

UNFINISHED BUSINESS

Library of Congress Cataloging-in-Publication Data

ISBN 1-887002-22-7
Brown, Ron
Ron Brown

UNFINISHED BUSINESS / Ron Brown
Published by ExHusker Press a Division of Cross Training
Publishing, Grand Island, Nebraska 68803

Distributed in the United States and Canada by Cross Training
Publishing

Edited by Gordon Thiessen
Editorial assistants: Sunny Robertson, Robyne Baker,
Cindy Messenger, Shane Petersen
Cover illustrator: Jeff Sharpton
Photo coordinator: Gordon Thiessen
Printed in the United States of America

For additional books and resources available
through ExHusker Press contact us at:

ExHusker Press
a Division of Cross Training Publishing
P.O. Box 1541
Grand Island, NE 68802

Contents

Introduction and Acknowledgments

Being a part of a National Championship football team was unquestionably a dream come true for me. There were incredible moments of glory and triumph after several years of Bowl losses. I am honored to be associated with Head Coach Tom Osborne, our football players, my fellow assistant coaches, all those associated with the team, the great Nebraska fans, and all the former Huskers who helped lay the foundation for this incredible season of "Unfinished Business."

The National Championship trophies, honors, rings, watches, celebrations, and paraphernalia provided great excitement and fellowship for the entire state of Nebraska and anyone else across America who leaped out of chairs claiming *victory* when fullback Cory Schlesinger bolted into the end zone for the game-winner.

Nevertheless, when I was asked to write this book regarding this sensational season, my heart, mind, and pen, began to gravitate toward the *journey* to victory, rather than the victory itself. While I attempted to gather relevant football facts regarding the season, I often found myself thinking about life off the gridiron—the *untold story* that you wouldn't find in a sports page or magazine. Life was not put on hold during our quest for the National Championship. As a matter of fact, as I started writing this book with my left hand, I would often hold my baby daughter, Sojourner, born February 18, 1995, in my right arm. As I so often looked into her dependent eyes, I couldn't help but be reminded that there are no time outs in the game of life. This book covers slightly over a year span. It is not merely about football—but life. Not merely my life—but in a sense, yours, too.

I'm sure you'll remember the exciting moments during this campaign to be No. 1. However, as you read this book, you will see that the most meaningful touchdowns were the serious issues that stirred people's hearts forever. Some of the issues that I share in this book include character, God, birth, violence, abortion, frustration, the death penalty, fear, sickness, racism, tragedy, incredible comebacks, meeting dignitaries, and oh yeah, football.

As you read this book, you may experience some of the same thoughts and emotions that I encountered while writing: tears, smiles, confusion, triumph, and most importantly introspection into your own heart.

Please understand—this account of the 1994 season of "Unfinished Business" is from my perspective. This book's views and opinions do not necessarily represent our Husker football team, Tom Osborne, our players, or the University of Nebraska at large.

I wrote this book as a private citizen who happens to be the receivers' coach for the Nebraska Cornhusker football team; and a Christian—one who desires to represent and honor the Lord Jesus Christ.

A number of our key players, personnel and contributors to this great season are not mentioned in this book. Many of the young men I personally coach are highlighted, because I work more closely with them. Therefore, this certainly is not the *whole* story. It is one person's account of a most dramatic season.

Even though this book is from my vantage point, there were many who contributed immeasurably to this work. Proverbs 15:22 states, "Without counsel purposes are disappointed: but in the multitude of counselors they are established."

My wife, Molvina, gives me the greatest human counsel that I know. Her passion for truth, sensitivity, and detail serves as a great check and balance for this book and my life in general. She is a woman of great character and helped shoulder this time-consuming project through pregnancy and childbirth. In addition, I thank my daughter, Sojourner, for reminding me of my priorities. I extend my appreciation to publisher, Gordon Thiessen, for his confidence in me.

I would also like to thank the following contributors for their tireless efforts of editing and support: Robyne Baker, Bill Doleman, Linda Ganzel, Dan and Cheryl Hauge, John and Penne Hanus, Bob and Maria Knowles, Cindy Messenger, Tom Osborne, Shane Petersen, Orv Qualsett, Sonny Robertson, and Terri Thiessen.

I acknowledge my sister, Theresa Brown, who shares with me a great source of inspiration for my life: our parents—Arthur and Pearl Brown, both deceased, home with the Lord.

Lastly in this section, but first in my heart, I acknowledge and thank my Savior and Lord, Jesus, who has given me purpose and meaning in life that not even a National Championship can provide.

Ron Brown
Assistant Football Coach
University of Nebraska

1

Preseason
Unfinished
Business

*W*hat a night! January 1, 1994, was a night I had dreamed of ever since I started watching college football in 1965 as an eight-year-old in Vineyard Haven, Massachusetts. I distinctly remember my dad and I watching games together on television—particularly the Bowl games on New Year's Day.

One New Year's Day, Dad took me to my uncle's house to watch Michigan State play UCLA in the Rose Bowl. What a great game! Michigan State had just finished a great regular season. I was rooting for them because their quarterback, Jimmy Raye, was my hero. State scored a touchdown late in the fourth quarter to make the score UCLA 14, Michigan State 12. State was going for the two-point conversion to tie, but on an option going right, Jimmy Raye pitched the ball to his halfback who was tackled short of the goal line. Disappointment set in. The greatest disappointment of the evening, however, was still on the horizon. As the Orange Bowl game was about to come on, Dad said it was time to go home, because we had school the next day. After we got home, I asked him if I could still watch the game on TV. He said, "No! Time for bed. School tomorrow." Talk about devastation—it was *one* of my all time lows. Sadly, I missed the Orange Bowl.

So, when I say January 1, 1994, was a dream come true, it really was...to be coaching in the Orange Bowl. Playing Florida State for the National Championship was something

I thought could only be a television dream, even though it wasn't my first bowl game. It was actually the seventh in as many years as I had coached at Nebraska. It was also my fourth Orange Bowl. I was 0-6 in bowl games at Nebraska. I was beginning to wonder if I was the culprit.

This year was different. Our 1993 season consisted of several tight situations and a number of comebacks en route to an undefeated regular season. We were ranked No. 1 in the nation going into the 1994 Orange Bowl against No. 2 Florida State. It was clearly the National Championship game. When our kicker, Byron Bennett, booted the field goal with 1:16 left in the game, putting us ahead 16-15, pure bedlam ripped across our sideline. It appeared to be an uncontrollable situation. Players were running out to the field from our sideline, screaming, hugging, and pointing at the Florida State sideline. Being excited is one thing, but losing total control is quite another.

The situation reminded me of our sideline back in 1990 when we played Colorado on an icy night in Lincoln. Mickey Joseph hit Johnny Mitchell for a touchdown pass, putting us up 12-0 in the third quarter. Our players were everywhere, screaming uncontrollably to the point where we were penalized. To this day, I believe we thought it was too good to be true to pull ahead of Colorado by two scores. In my opinion it was a lack of confidence. Colorado's Eric Bienemy proceeded to score four touchdowns in the fourth quarter to hand us a very bitter loss.

Even though our 1993 team was better than our 1990 team in most areas, I still believe we lacked the poise and confidence at the end of that 1994 Orange Bowl to get it done. We were good enough—just not quite confident enough.

On the ensuing kickoff, we booted it out of bounds to give Florida State good field position on their own 35-yard line with the great Charlie Ward at quarterback and a dangerous corps of receivers. With a combination of passes, runs, and Nebraska penalties, Florida State marched deep inside our territory and kicked the go-ahead field goal, making the score Florida State 18, Nebraska 16. Our offense made a gallant effort, as Tommie Frazier hit Trumane Bell with a pass that gave us a chance to attempt a 48-yard field goal on the last play of the game. But alas, it went wide left. As painful as it was, I joined several Florida State and Nebraska players at mid-field for a post-game prayer. God deserved the glory and thanks even more than we deserved the National Championship.

A month or so later, I was offered the wide receivers coaching job at Florida State University by Bobby Bowden. John Eason, their former wide receivers coach had left to become the Assistant Head Coach at South Carolina.

I shared with Coach Osborne that FSU was interested in me. I wasn't sure what I wanted to do. My admiration, respect, and love for Tom was unparalleled. As far as I was concerned, I had the best job in America and the one that God had in store for me at that moment. It's hard to imagine working for a more loyal man than Tom Osborne. Yet the decision wouldn't be an easy one.

I believed from a pure football standpoint the move to Florida State might enhance my résumé. Florida State had a different type of offensive system. I had been a coach in a power, option-run, play-action passing system. Florida State would provide a more wide open drop-back passing attack. Combined with my early years of coaching defense and administrative experience as Assistant to the Athletic Director, it would round out my experience and possibly enhance my position on the proverbial ladder of success. But there was something missing in this line of thought...what did God want me to do?

My wife, Molvina, and I talked it through and both collectively and individually prayed about it often. You see, I am a Christian. My life has been paid for by Jesus Christ. My life belongs to Him. Therefore, I can't do what "I" want to do. I must do what "He" wants me to do.

As I study the Bible, and try, and fail in this world, I am coming to the conclusion that God basically expects one thing of me—to yield my life to Him and to conform to the likeness of Jesus Christ. It is whether or not I have Christ-like character that concerns Him most. Simply put, God's goal for me is to become more like Jesus Christ.

To one who isn't a Christian this may make little sense. I know when I first trusted my life to Jesus as Savior and Lord it made zero sense to me. Now, 15 years and hundreds of broken and fulfilled dreams later, I'm beginning to understand what David meant when he wrote Psalm 27:4, "One thing have I desired of the Lord; that I will seek after; that I may dwell in the house of the Lord all the days of my life, to behold the beauty of the Lord, and to inquire in his temple." Only one thing was important.

I didn't have to grab God by the collar with two hands and shake out his specific will for me. Nor did I need to make plane reservations to Tibet to climb to the top of a high Himalayan mountain to hear some dramatic piece of information. Paying close attention to God means seeing *what* He is doing in this world, *where* He is doing it, and *who* He is doing it with. His main purpose is to draw men and women to a relationship with His Son, Jesus Christ.

As I saw what God was doing in my life and who He was doing it with, it became much clearer to me where, at least for now, He wanted me to do it. What was "it?" It was inspiring people to know Jesus as their Savior and Lord through the platform of coaching. God had blessed me in Nebraska with Christian camps for disadvantaged children, a Christian radio ministry, and a writing and speaking platform.

As I thought about the ministry that God entrusted to me in Nebraska, I didn't sense a peace about leaving it yet.

Not only did I sense an urgency in my heart to continue, I experienced a great *desire* to stay. Psalm 37:4 says, "Delight yourself in the Lord and He will give you the desires of your heart." I believe this verse means if I delight in God's goal for me to conform to the likeness of Jesus Christ through great intimacy and fellowship that only the Holy Spirit can produce, then God will start shaping my desires to reflect His.

So, Florida State or Nebraska? I felt Nebraska seeping through my veins, my consciousness. My heart leaped for joy when I thought about staying. I thought about the children I had spent summers with on the Omaha Nation Indian Reservation in Macy, Nebraska. I thought about how much I loved them and wanted them to know Jesus Christ. I thought about Tom Osborne, my receivers and fellow coaches, the fans, and the wonderful people I've met across the state of Nebraska. I sensed what God's will was for me. My role was to continue at Nebraska.

As I awoke on the morning of the press conference to announce the decision, I saw thick snowflakes coming down like pillows. I whispered to my California-bred wife, "It's not too late to go to the beach," referring to Tallahassee, Florida.

Molvina whispered back, "The snow doesn't look too bad to me." I had to admit it was the best snowfall I had ever seen. Yeah, buddy, there was still "unfinished business" at Nebraska.

2

First Quarter
Looking for
More in '94

*T*he 1994 year of "unfinished business" got off to quite a strange start for me. I noticed something different about my starting wingback, Abdul Muhammad. Abdul led our team in receptions in 1993, and he would be heavily relied on as the "go-to" receiver his senior year. Abdul was a small receiver physically, at 5' 9", 160 pounds, but his heart was at least 6' 9" and 260 pounds.

Just a year prior, in July of 1993, while home for summer break in Compton, California, Abdul was the victim of a drive-by shooting, as he innocently entered a car. With a potentially fatal bullet lodged in his buttock, there was a real question whether he would be able to perform. Amazingly, with the bullet still inside, he battled back and was able to play in our opener against North Texas.

At about mid-year, Abdul was playing very well. ESPN interviewed Abdul with the intention of doing a story on him as an inner-city youngster from a gang-infested community, who had overcome great obstacles to become a big-time college football player. However, the interview turned out to be a bogus account of Abdul's alleged membership in the Piru Bloods Gang. Abdul and his mother, Henrietta, denied his membership in any gang and protested the story, with the University of Nebraska's backing. ESPN later made a public apology to both Abdul and the University of Nebraska.

With all of the pressure and hype of that story, Abdul demonstrated tremendous mental toughness and had a great game against Kansas State following the ESPN incident. Abdul continued as one of the best third down clutch receivers in college football and had a streak of catching at least one pass in every game starting in the previous year's Orange Bowl.

In the 1994 Orange Bowl, Abdul kept the streak alive with a catch early in the game but suffered a game-ending injury on the next play, as he took a devastating shot from a Florida State defensive back that cracked his ribs and lacerated his liver. He was immediately hospitalized, and there was great concern once again for his physical well-being.

After healing, I noticed that Abdul would uncharacteristically take himself out of certain scrimmage plays during our 1994 spring football practices. He didn't seem to have the same tenacity. I sensed that he felt unsure if he was physically ready yet. I didn't pressure him. I knew how Abdul loved football, and that he had always shown great effort in practice. It was obvious, even though he had the medical okay to practice, that he had to work out some things on his own. However, I had to admit I was a little nervous about him. He was the only returning starter in the receiving corps for 1994.

The summer of 1994 came with many of our players working out hard while attending summer school. Abdul hit us with a bomb—he wanted to redshirt. He was one of our few players that didn't redshirt as a freshman. His skills and his tremendous intelligence on the field, despite his diminutive stature, were such that we played him as a freshman back in 1991. Coach Osborne and I shared with Abdul our policy of redshirting freshmen if they so desire, but not upperclassmen who are major contributors unless there is an injury limitation or severe academic problem. The doctors had cleared Abdul to play and academically he was on target to graduate. After serious thought, Abdul decided to play. I breathed a sigh of relief.

There was another incredible piece of news for Molvina and I that summer. We conceived our first baby—a little God-sent bundle of joy. We could hardly wait.

Coach Osborne made a decision that was more difficult than most people imagine—to have an optional coaching staff devotional to start every day. It would last usually two or three minutes and consist of Tom asking if any coach had a verse from the Bible or any other comment he would like to share. After 30 seconds or a minute reciting a verse, we would all be silent and do whatever we wanted—pray, silently read, or think for a brief moment. Coach would usually end that devotional with an "Amen" and start our work for the day with everyone present.

In a day and age when Christianity and outward religious gestures are being attacked, I appreciated Tom's direction on this issue. The idea was not to force anything on anyone. It was optional and what was said by any coach could be anything that was on his heart. It gave each of us an opportunity to at least pause and think about God and how He related to our work and our personal lives.

My general impressions going into the 1994 season were very optimistic just after the Orange Bowl. Even though we'd lost, I really believed we would, in many respects, be the team to beat in college football in 1994. I sensed a surge of determination from our players during the off-season that coincided with our motto, "Unfinished Business." Of the players I was coaching, I was very pleased that the three top tight ends, in particular, pushed themselves hard. Matt Shaw, a tenacious blocker, flat out-works everyone. Eric Alford, a former wingback, made the transition to tight end better than I expected. Eric is blessed with great speed and explosive ability and in spring practice showed he could be a very dangerous deep threat. Mark Gilman, an unassuming but much improved player, had excellent hands. I thought Eric and Mark would be just what the doctor ordered as a dual receiving threat. That, combined with Matt's blocking ability, would make the tight end position one of the strengths of the team.

I have to admit, I wasn't as confident with the wide receiver situation. I personally grieved the graduation of last year's heart and soul of "the itty-bitty committee," Corey Dixon. Corey, now in the NFL, was a great competitor whose performance seemed to improve when the pressure was on. Even though Abdul had decided to play, I still wasn't quite sure if his heart was really in it. I saw an apathy towards football in him that was not present before. I spent a lot of time on the phone with his mother, Henrietta. I noticed that she, too, was concerned for Abdul.

I've always been pleased with our second wingback, Clester Johnson. He was a steady performer who had an excellent 1993 sophomore season as a physical blocker and short-range receiver. I was so proud of Clester—a highly recruited quarterback from Bellevue West High School, who was the Nebraska High School Athlete of the Year. His many talents created big expectations. It didn't work out for Clester at quarterback as a freshman. He bounced around a little as a defensive back and finally ended up as a wingback. There were times when I know he was doubting himself. I was secretly hoping that Clester would end up with me. I saw him in the mold of Rich Bell, Nate Turner, and Vincent Hawkins in terms of being a strong, heavy duty blocker at the wingback position.

Clester's confidence and tenacity improved drastically, and he became an unsung but very valuable player as a wingback. Along with Abdul, he gave us a nice combination of a pure downfield receiver and a punishing perimeter blocker.

Reggie Baul was a big play speedster with nice hands. Riley Washington was one of the fastest humans in the United States, already a two-time NCAA All-American in the 100-meter dash for our track team. Together with John Livingston, a sure-handed junior-college transfer, they gave us a nice blend of speed, hands, and route running ability at the split end position. However, as a group, the blocking consistency we needed for a good option attack was lacking during spring football.

Brendan Holbein, an initial walk-on player from Cozad, Nebraska, would have to play a key role in our perimeter run offense. Formerly a wingback, he moved to split end because he was a tremendous blocker. Though not very big, he could bench press over 300 hundred pounds and was a fierce competitor with a lot of pride in what he did. I first noticed his blocking toughness when he was a redshirted freshman. Of that group of split ends, Baul, Washington, and Livingston, Holbein was the least fluid as a pass route runner. But he was sure-handed, very smart, and a reliable blocker. Brendan made that transition look easy, and our option game in fall camp looked much better with him at split end than without him during spring ball. Yet, he still was a relatively unknown commodity in game-like experience. With Abdul's uncertainty and with his influence on the wide receivers, I felt they did not prepare as well during the summer.

There was an even more pressing matter that really rocked my insides, but it had nothing to do with football. One early morning before staff meetings began, I was visited by a woman who said she was from New Jersey and was a close friend of Harold Lamont Otey. Otey was on death row in Nebraska for the rape and murder of a woman in the 1970s. His execution was scheduled for August, just a short time away. She brought up the issue of Otey's death sentence and wanted to know if I would be willing to make public statements on behalf of eradicating the death penalty—particularly regarding Otey. I told her I wasn't sure how I felt about the death penalty. However, in light of the fast approaching execution, I felt a sense of urgency to see Otey.

I had often thought about Otey while he was on death row. I wondered if he would be open to hearing about Jesus. I wasn't concerned who told him, I just wanted him to go to heaven. Therefore, I used the opportunity to ask this woman if she could get me in to visit. She asked me why. I told her I was a Christian and wanted to share my faith with him. She said she would try. A few days later, I was told she had personally contacted Otey, and he was not interested in any Christian trying to convert him. I was disappointed, but I immediately asked if I could see him anyway without sharing my faith. I sincerely cared about what he was about to go through. The message of Christ on the cross is foolishness to non-Christians, but power to those who believe as the Apostle Paul states in 1 Corinthians, chapter 1. I still wanted to extend the love of Christ to Otey, as one who cared and had compassion. Someone once said, "Always preach Christ, use words when necessary." I didn't have to preach to him, just love him with compassion and sincerity. God could use even that. Otey's friend finally called me back and declined my offer. The night of Otey's execution was a very emotional one for me. I was deeply grieved as I watched the televised proceedings at the State Penitentiary in Lincoln. There were signs and interviews, some showing great exuberance over Otey's upcoming death. Because I believe there is a heaven and hell and Jesus' statement, "That no man comes to the Father (God) but by me (Jesus)," I ached deeply when Harold Otey was pronounced dead above the sickening cheers.

That execution interrupted my preoccupation with our football season. A few weeks later, I received a letter from Otey's friend in New Jersey. It was a blistering account of anger, as she ripped me up one side and down the other. In short, she thought it was completely futile to share my Christian faith with Otey, and unforgivable that I didn't voice support for the eradication of the death sentence for him. She also accused me of being insensitive to a fellow black brother at the mercy of a racist penal system. I never thought the penal system was entirely just and I did appreciate that she, a white woman, had compassion for Otey and other blacks who are on death row in this country. Yet, he was proven guilty of rape and murder. At this moment, I am not sure whether justice is best served with the death penalty or not. I *am* sure, however, there is life after death. I believe I was offering my best to Otey by seeking an opportunity to share Jesus with him. I believe, given the option of sharing my faith with him or saying something to the media in opposition to the death penalty, the former would have the greatest impact. Otey's friend, and I'm sure many others, would beg to differ with me.

In the off-season, we were invited to play in both the Pigskin Classic in Anaheim, California, and the Kickoff Classic in East Rutherford, New Jersey. Coach Osborne asked the entire team to vote on playing in one or none of the games. The majority of the players voted on the Kickoff Classic if we could play West Virginia, the only other 1993 undefeated regular season team besides us. Many felt that West Virginia got the short end of the stick by not being able to play us in the Orange Bowl for the national title. Therefore, in a sense this would be the unofficial title game— retroactive, one might say.

It's always a challenge to get ready for an early game. I have mixed emotions about it. You do get to play on national TV, which can turn out to be a good recruiting tool, provided you win. If you lose, it is better to lose early than late in the season in terms of the polls. I've always had a concern, however, of adding games to an already long season. These young men have great pressure on them already with a rigorous training schedule and academic demands. At the same time, they are the focus of attention by the entire state of Nebraska. With a very experienced quarterback, Tommie Frazier, returning, we felt the percentages would favor us and give us a game under our belts before we had to play scrappy Texas Tech in Lubbock. It was our third Kickoff Classic, and in each case we started the game with a quarterback that had at least two years experience: Turner Gill in 1983 against Penn State, and Steve Taylor in 1988 against Texas A & M. We won both games.

The trip to the New York area brought back nice memories. Just 11 years ago in this city, I first met Molvina at a Super Bowl party. Molvina and I miss certain things about New York—the walks, canoe riding in Central Park, jogging together across the George Washington Bridge, the great museums, unique culture and Calvary Church services. However, this was a trip Molvina could not make. She was bed-ridden because of her pregnancy.

Reading between the lines of the newspaper accounts of West Virginia's preseason progress, I sensed that on paper we had the advantage because we had greater team depth. Nevertheless, I was fairly anxious about the game. There were the usual first game concerns regarding smoothness, concentration, and preparation.

In addition, newly passed NCAA legislation limited Division 1-A football teams like us from bringing in more than 105 players. Because of our high repetition practice philosophy and consequential reliance on numerous scout and varsity team players, those 105 had to take up the slack. We had exhausting practices, particularly for the position that probably runs the most in practice, receivers. I was taking great measures to make sure their legs were not over-trained. My philosophy in coaching receivers has always been to stretch their motor skills and techniques such as a diverse set of catching drills, but have minimal sprint action for their legs. What they get in a normal practice is plenty in my opinion. "Over-trained" legs mean tired legs that are sluggish when they play and also very susceptible to injury. "Over-trained hands" and technical skills are beneficial for finely tuned, precision reactions.

I excuse receivers from running extra sprints with the rest of the team after practice, but I will work extra coordination, precision feet, and hand-eye drills with a football with seldom a day off. I spend time praying to God about knowing when to push an athlete and when to back off. My personality is one that pushes and challenges, and so I have sought God's wisdom to make sure I balance that correctly with fun type activities after practice.

The receivers worked hard in practice. Even two days before the game, and with the limited numbers, they ran very hard. I was hoping they would not be weary-legged. We opened up the game with a nice drive on offense. Abdul looked sharp, running a nice hook route, with Tommie Frazier firing an accurate ball for a nice gain. With that catch, Abdul continued a long string of consecutive games where he caught at least one pass.

Later in the drive, however, disaster struck. Tommie ran a play-action pass and went to Clester Johnson on a deep square-out. It was a great throw, but Clester didn't seem to be ready for it. It went through his hands and, amazingly, into the hands of a West Virginia defensive back for an interception. Not only was it a tough break for our offense because it thwarted what looked like an easy scoring drive, but it was also one of my receivers who cost us. No one on earth is immune from mistakes. Clester Johnson shouldn't be condemned for his dropped ball. It was simply a mistake. But I admit I take it personally. That's what's tough. It's really an attitude of vanity—too much pride. When the receivers catch a pass, I secretly take some glory. When they drop it, I blame myself and then accuse others who criticize a receiver for dropping the ball as short-sided and negative—not noticing their blocking abilities enough. When receivers are catching the ball, I'm curious as to why they aren't given more credit, but I'm mad if they get too much credit because people may think it was a fluke or something.

Perhaps we struggle with seeking people's applause sometimes. When a receiver catches a football, he will usually get more applause than when he makes a key block. At times, to my frustration, I get caught up in that mentality. So when Clester dropped that ball my heart dropped like a shot put hitting the soft dirt. Just as I was praying to God on the sideline to help me have a mature perspective about the situation, Abdul dropped another perfect throw from Frazier that probably would have been a touchdown.

"Why me?" I complained. What could possibly happen next? Even though Matt Shaw had a great blocking game and Reggie Baul was named our offensive nominee for the Big Eight Player of the Week, not to mention that we won 31-0, I couldn't stop thinking about those two drops. One of the sports writers wanted to interview me after the game, not about the win or Reggie Baul's big day, but about the two drops. Talk about a thorn in my flesh. To top it off, we had a plane delay back to Lincoln so the entire team went back to the hotel in New Jersey to eat and rest.

For me, it was punishment to have to face everyone and the remarks from well-meaning fans about dropped passes. I tried to pray and ask God to give me perspective. The desire to receive applause from man can sure get in the way. There was something very positive about going back to the hotel to wait, however. I noticed that Abdul didn't seem to be upset about anything, although he wouldn't normally show it even if he was hurting. For the first time, I saw Clester without his "award winning" smile. I pulled him over to talk, and he shared with me how down he was about the dropped ball. It enabled me to share with him how valuable he was to me and to the team. More importantly, I was able to share my faith in Jesus Christ. Clester nodded and was very appreciative.

That was the first time I had shared with Clester that intimately. I wanted him to know that no matter how bad he felt and how much he doubted himself that God didn't doubt him. And that He has a great plan for his life. Romans 8:28

says, "that all things work together for the good for those who love the Lord for those who are called according to His purpose." I would say that a dropped ball, no matter how much it hurt, would be a part of "all things." A dropped ball gave me an opportunity to share my faith with Clester Johnson.

On the plane as we flew back to Nebraska, I was relieved to finally be able to open my Bible and seek God's intimate, tender love to me. It's funny, even with a 31-0 win, there are still hurts inside that only God can touch and heal. I found myself cherishing my relationship with Jesus Christ. I recalled that six years earlier, riding the team plane back from the 1988 Kickoff Classic after we had beaten a talented Texas A&M team, I had experienced almost the same dilemma. My star wingback, Dana Brinson, had dropped two passes in that game. One would have been an easy touchdown.

The thorn in my flesh was pricking me pretty good. Again, on the airplane, I opened my Bible for God's comfort and noticed that Nebraska's Governor at that time, Kay Orr, was sitting across the aisle from me with her Bible open. I shyly nodded to her. When I got home, I wrote her a note to tell her I appreciated her interest in reading God's Word. She wrote back, and to this day we share in Christian functions together. I've truly enjoyed my fellowship with God on airplanes.

Next was fiery Texas Tech in Lubbock, Texas. It would be an ESPN Thursday night game. We had a week and a half to prepare for it. Texas Tech would eventually share the Southwest Conference Championship and went on to play in the 1995 Cotton Bowl.

The night before the Tech game at the team hotel, I ran into Bob Knowles. Bob is an attorney in Omaha and has been a huge fan of Nebraska football since he was a kid in Omaha. Bob and I have developed a friendship over the years that includes his wife, Maria, and my wife, Molvina. He and Maria have three children, Christina, Bobby and Elaina.

Tragically, their fourth, Michael, died as an infant just a few months prior—a very tough time for Bob and Maria.

My greatest desire regarding Bob was for him to trust Jesus Christ as his Savior and Lord. In addition to football, Bob occasionally would ask many questions regarding my faith in God.

So that night in the team hotel when Bob and I saw each other, it was a golden opportunity for us to talk. I asked Bob if he would like to take a brisk walk with me while we talked because I hadn't worked out yet. We talked a little football, but this walk and talk would prove to challenge me far beyond our national title dreams.

The issue of life and death and what comes after became our main subject. Bob knew what I believed on the matter. I believe that each person's life did not start at birth but rather at conception. I believe God orchestrates that life by creating it through the sexual union of a man and woman. I believe this created life, no matter which side of the birth canal, is a life that is accountable to God. As a Christian, I believe that each person must make a decision about Jesus Christ, either to trust Him as Savior and Lord as the only means of spending eternity with God or to reject Him. I believe apathy or simply not making a decision counts as a rejection. I also believe in heaven and hell. Those who trust in Christ automatically have a home reserved in heaven. Those who reject Christ are hell-bound, unless before they die, they come to a trusting knowledge that Jesus is what He claimed to be. By the way, I believe hell is a *real* place.

Before you start thinking what kind of an opinionated jerk I am, please know that most of what I just stated were answers to questions fired at me from the inquisitive Bob Knowles. He sure challenges me sometimes because he asks simple, yet penetrating, questions that cause me to think about what I believe. Was my belief just an opinion, or did it have biblical justification, and could I articulate more clearly this faith that I have banked my life on?

However, on this warm night while we walked and talked, I wanted to turn the tables and challenge Bob also. I asked him what he believed. Bob told me he believed everything I had just stated to him. The best thing I heard him say was that he believed Jesus died for his sins personally and only through trusting Christ could he go to heaven. I was overjoyed to hear he had trusted in Jesus as Savior and Lord.

The conversation got sadder as we walked. He talked about Michael's death and how that had affected Maria, him, and their three other children. We agreed that Michael was in heaven with God. That incident really drew Bob and his wife closer to the Lord. Bob shared that before Michael's death he had always intellectually believed in Jesus, but that after Michael's brief life he now had a personal and complete relationship with Christ.

There is a scripture in the Bible that lead me to believe infants do go to heaven after death. In 2 Samuel chapter 12, a son was born out of the adulterous act of David and Bathsheba. The child died on his seventh day and David made the statement in verse 23 of that chapter, "Can I bring him back again? I shall go to him but he shall not return to me." I believe Bob will return to Michael one day when he dies. Also, as a footnote from that same verse, it implies that Michael will not return to Bob, which teaches that reincarnation does not exist. We also talked about Harold Lamont Otey and the death penalty. Certainly it was a very meaningful walk that was an answer to prayer. Not only did I grow closer to a friend, but I also found a new brother in Christ.

The Texas Tech game went very well for us with a convincing win. But there was a key loss within this win. Mike Minter, our outstanding free safety, tore ligaments in his knee and was out for the season. It was a tough blow for our team, our defense in particular. However, converted quarterback Tony Veland, who had suffered a season-ending knee injury the year before, rose to the occasion and was playing very well at safety. For me personally, this game was another of ups and downs. We felt we could strike quick on Texas Tech. Early in the game we ran an option fake and deep throw. Sure enough, Reggie Baul executed a nice release on Tech's cornerback who was slightly fooled. Tommie threw what I thought was a well-executed pass that could have been a touchdown. Reggie had to reach high for the ball, but I thought his hands were not in the best position to catch it. He didn't hang on and neither did my emotions. I shook my head in disbelief, and as far as I was concerned, the curse was still on. In addition, Clester missed a key block early in the game on a big third-down play that forced us to punt.

As in the West Virginia game, some good things took place, too. Brendan Holbein sustained a block on the cornerback that seemed to last forever and helped Tommie Frazier to ramble on a long touchdown run early in the game. It was also great to see Eric Alford get in the act as he caught his first touchdown pass of the year. It was a real confidence booster for Eric.

However, there was another negative. Near the end of the game while we were holding on to a comfortable lead we realized Abdul hadn't caught a pass yet. Coach Osborne has always been good about doing something nice for an individual, provided it doesn't embarrass the opponent. It's tough to throw when you are way ahead, but Coach Osborne decided on a short throw to Abdul to continue his pass-catching streak. Unfortunately, the pass was too high and was intercepted. We did get the ball back shortly thereafter, but Coach Osborne was through throwing the ball. Hence, Abdul's streak of catching at least one pass in each consecutive game was finally broken and with it, his spirit. He refused to talk after the game as I tried to explain the circumstances. We were two wins and no losses with UCLA a week and a half away. I had to concentrate on the positives.

Fireworks were planned in Memorial Stadium to introduce our new Husker Vision and big play screens the night before our first home game against UCLA. Fireworks of a different sort struck the night after the Tech game back in Lincoln. We decided as a coaching staff to practice the players the day after the Texas Tech game on Friday, and then give them Saturday and Sunday off. Everybody showed up to practice except Abdul. As practice began without him, I began wondering what was going on with him. I knew he was upset because his string had been broken, but I couldn't imagine him missing practice. There are consequences for missing practice without an excuse. I had some strange emotions about it. Part of me felt that Abdul had an attitude problem, influencing some of the other receivers in a negative way. However, another side of me said that Abdul really loved football and wanted to win. He had always been a great competitor in practice and games and was just going through a difficult time. This situation was breaking my heart because I loved Abdul and didn't know how to reach him.

The next day, I finally touched base with Abdul. He admitted that he was very disappointed about his catching streak coming to an end and about the limited balls he had been given the opportunity to catch. I listened to him intently because he was facing a common problem. Sometimes we don't get what we feel we deserve, compared to others. Maybe we don't get the promotion on our job we thought we deserved or the attention from our friends. We've all been through it before, and I think Abdul was having a bout with the same thing. Abdul was smart enough to know that he didn't have control over everything that takes place.

That realization was one of the best things that ever happened to me. When I was coaching at Brown University in 1986, I was called by Howard Schnellenberger, then the head coach at Louisville, about an assistant coaching position that Jim Caldwell, present Wake Forest Head Coach, had just left.

Caldwell told me he was going to recommend me for that position. I have to admit I was excited, but was very surprised just a few days later when Coach Schnellenberger called me. He asked me several questions about my background and coaching experience. He then said good-bye and that he might get back to me.

There was so much more I wanted to say, so much more I could have said. I felt like I blew it. I talked to Caldwell later. He had just taken the receivers job at Penn State, and I asked if he thought Coach Schnellenberger would interview me. Based on what I told Caldwell, he felt that Schnellenberger *did* interview me over the phone.

As I moped around for a day or so thinking that I blew it, a Christian friend, seeing my sadness, shared Proverbs 21:1, "The king's heart is in the hand of the Lord; He directs it like a watercourse wherever He pleases." I have to tell you reading that verse was like a piano lifted off my back. It was God who controlled the "king's heart," in this case, Coach Schnellenberger. It was God who would direct his heart if He wanted me at Louisville. As a Christian, this was the medicine the doctor ordered. I didn't have to control the circumstances or the people around me. I just had to be faithful and let God take care of the rest.

When Coach Schnellenberger hired someone else, I wasn't upset. I believe that God had another plan. A year later, when Coach Osborne hired me at Nebraska, I could see Proverbs 21:1 coming full circle. I knew that God used that verse, with the rejection, to teach me a great spiritual truth.

Abdul quietly went back to his football responsibility. We disciplined him for missing practice and told him he would not start against UCLA. When a first-teamer is demoted from his starting position for the game it can be embarrassing for him. It hits the newspapers and is particularly evident at a nationally televised contest like UCLA. In addition, I had gotten wind that Abdul's mom and brother, Shadid, were planning to surprise him by flying in from Los Angeles to see the game. I think mother Muhammad, Shadid, and I all breathed a sigh of relief when Abdul decided to return to the team.

I mentioned there was a different sort of fireworks on that infamous Friday night after the Texas Tech game. Our players are like most college students on the weekend—they like to get out to social gatherings, parties, and such. Times certainly have changed. What used to be a fist fight when tensions got high at such gatherings has dangerously evolved into gunfire. The problem with gun shots is that they can strike innocent bystanders such as the case with Abdul in 1993.

The second potentially fatal shooting of an innocent bystander on our football team took place this particular Friday night. For the second time this innocent bystander was one of my receivers; this time it was Brendan Holbein. Can you imagine that? What a world!

I must admit this seldom happens in Lincoln, Nebraska, still one of the safer cities in America. Young people across our nation are exposed to this dangerous culture continually. We, the United States of America, are statistically the most violent nation on earth today. Abdul Muhammad and Brendan Holbein are just a couple of examples of the war zone we live in. The stray bullet grazed Brendan's abdominal area and would cost him a few days of practice. However, I was just pleased this young man was not dead or seriously wounded.

The fireworks display the night before the UCLA game was spectacular. The new sound system and Husker Vision big-screens were introduced to our team and approximately 35,000 fans. It was a very emotional night for the players. Our first home game against a nationally ranked, undefeated UCLA team would be a big barometer in our quest for the national title.

UCLA's great wide receiver, J. J. Stokes, was injured in its opener against Tennessee and would not play against us. However, with the "other" receiver, Kevin Jordan, nearly as dangerous as Stokes, UCLA was a very potent offensive football team. It had a good running game to go along with quarterback, Wayne Cook, at the helm.

Our offense played brilliantly. At times, I can tell early in the contest if it will be a dominating offensive game for us by watching the blocking tenacity and explosion of our offensive line, fullbacks, tight ends, and wide receivers. I was concerned about Brendan Holbein—how tenacious would he be as a blocker? He couldn't block all week during practice because of the heavy stitching in his torso from the gunshot wound. His perimeter blocking had been sensational in the first two games. For our option attack to really go, Holbein would have to be at full strength by game time.

First impressions are often important in life and it is usually the case in a football game as well. I anxiously watched Brendan on our first offensive play. To my delight, on a play that went away from his side, he went after the nearest defensive back. I soon realized that ol' Brendan didn't have a tenacity problem. He hit that defensive back so hard the poor lad was up-ended, legs straight in the air, body exploding to the turf. It was a brutal blow. As Holbein got up with energy and vigor, I knew the day belonged to him. He had set the tone for a perimeter onslaught, as he put on quite a blocking display. He also caught two passes—one in the fourth quarter was a shovel pass in which he eluded the defender nicely en route to his first career touchdown. It was the finishing touch to a great afternoon of offensive football for the Huskers.

Everyone was a star! The offensive line, nicknamed the "Pipeline," was clearly dominating inside. All-American Tackle Zach Wiegert put on a "clinic," showing great agility in the open field, blocking the perimeter as he pulled on our counter-sweep plays. I must admit I've always secretly wanted that big guy as a tight end. He can run, jump, block, and catch. He bounces around like a 10-year-old on a trampoline.

Our fullback, Cory Schlesinger, was really coming into his own as both a vicious blocker and dangerous inside runner. Assistant Head Coach Frank Solich, who coaches our running backs, had patiently believed that Cory would rise to the occasion. I-back Lawrence Phillips, was clearly one of the top four or five backs in America. His toughness and consistency along with his break-away speed gave our offense great big play ability. He is also a fine receiver and we took advantage of that with quick screen passes to him.

Tight end Eric Alford with his electrifying speed once again found the end zone, as the recipient of another touchdown pass from Heisman candidate Tommie Frazier to open our scoring in the UCLA game. Unsung Matt Shaw consistently won battle after battle at tight end against UCLA's defensive ends and linebackers. Clester Johnson had a big blocking day—at times maintaining perimeter blocks five to six seconds long.

Even though he was not allowed to start the game, Abdul had a nice day. His highlight was a pretty wingback reverse where he scampered for 32 yards. Combine all of this with Reggie Baul's speed outside for the potential deep balls and we looked like an offensive unit with too many weapons to stop.

The key, of course, was quarterback Tommie Frazier. Tommie was having a big year. He was running the show brilliantly. This game answered many questions and concerns. We were over the hump from a difficult week of concerns. It was almost too good to be true. Frazier complained about a little soreness in his calf, but it didn't seem to be a big deal. We were on our way!

While preparing for Pacific, the coaching staff knew this would be our toughest challenge. Beating three tough opponents on national TV and then having to play a team where we were a 50-point favorite, and not on TV, was going to be a motivational chore. What really helped us this season was the mission our kids were on. We had come so close in the Orange Bowl against Florida State. We knew we couldn't stub our toe with an upset. However, there was one other mechanism that served as a built-in motivation—the AP poll (sports writers) and the coaches' poll (Division 1-A head coaches).

We've always told our players not to worry about the polls; rather, they should just concentrate on playing their best. Hopefully, we'll win them all. No guarantee, but the best chances result from playing your best. I must admit that this year the polls served to our advantage. I view them as a pesky dog always nipping at our heels, not allowing us to slow down at all. Going into the Pacific game, we realized that not only did we need to win, but we needed to win big.

Our poll nemesis all year was Penn State which possessed one of the most explosive offensive units in college football history. They were scoring big and winning impressively. A ho-hum win by us could allow Penn State to take the No. 1 spot and win the hearts of the national media (who has great influence over the poll voters). Going into the Bowl season, we needed to be in the No. 1 spot because we wouldn't play Penn State in a Bowl if we were both undefeated. Consequently, we could lose the title at the polls.

There is a fine line when you start playing for the polls. Coach Osborne was not going to deliberately embarrass an opponent by running up the score. If we got way ahead, he would start removing the first and second unit players.

Thursday's practice was held inside the Cook Pavilion because of inclement weather. Something strange took place that would create this season's greatest drama. Tommie Frazier began to limp noticeably about midway through practice. We knew that a slight soreness in his calf muscle had developed in the UCLA game, but the practice sessions since then had shown no apparent injury. Tommie ran well all week. It was a concern to the coaching staff because it was a mystery injury. Why would Tommie run well through the week and then start noticeably limping halfway through practice on Thursday?

Tommie couldn't even explain it himself. He thought he might have been hit there against UCLA but wasn't sure. What was this mystery injury? Nothing seemed to show up medically after a thorough examination. Early in the Pacific game, Tommie's calf acted up again. Coach Osborne decided not to mess with it anymore and made a replacement—back-up quarterback Brook Berringer.

A little over a year ago, in the 1993 season opener against North Texas, Brook found himself in the same scenario. Tommie suffered an ankle sprain on the first play of the game and Brook entered that game and had a big day, directing our offense and completing every pass. In our minds, there was no question that the tall, quiet outdoorsman from Goodland, Kansas, could get the job done against Pacific. Sure enough, Brook was sharp. In addition to running our offense well, he threw for three touchdown passes, a couple of soft touch throws. He hit Eric Alford on a bomb for one of the scores where Eric really displayed his great speed, out-running Pacific's secondary, as Brook laid it right in there. It was great to see Clester catch his first touchdown pass of the year. Clester released around his defender after Brook ran down the line on an option action fake. Brook then floated a soft one over the defender's head to the striding Clester for an easy six.

Coach Osborne is truly remarkable when it comes to juggling all the aspects of game day. In addition to being the head coach and offensive coordinator calling the plays, he seems to have a great feel for which players need to get more involved in the offense. He knew that Abdul needed a boost.

We were way ahead in the score late in the second half. It was time to "call off the dogs." Yet the best way to get Abdul a big play for his confidence (which would be crucial later in the season), without embarrassing Pacific Coach Chuck Shelton and his team, was to throw a short pass in front of the defensive back and let Abdul do the rest.

Coach Osborne called the play, but changed the read on it. Normally, on this particular pass, the first read would be to go to the split end on the other side away from Abdul. Tom told the receiver bringing the play into the huddle to tell Brook to throw it to Abdul—something Tom doesn't do that often. He must have sensed it was the thing to do in this case. Sure enough, Brook fired a quick pass to Abdul in front of the defensive back, and man, did Abdul do the rest! His spin move outside toward the sideline after the catch reminded me of NBA star Hakeem Olajuwon's patented "quick spin" with his back to the defender and then on to the big dunk. Abdul jetted by the defensive back with great quickness and didn't blow the dunk. He left his feet at about the 3-yard line and extended the ball over the plane of the goal line just before his momentum carried him out of bounds.

It was a beautiful sight as the official brought both arms straight up in the air. As teammates cheered Abdul for his first touchdown of the season, I couldn't forget the compassion and wisdom of that tall, red-headed fellow who calls the plays. Perhaps Tom remembered Abdul's disappointment at Texas Tech. I know he wasn't happy with Abdul's reactions to that disappointment, but Tom is certainly a forgiving and sensitive individual. That little "insignificant" touchdown play Tom Osborne called in a blow-out game against Pacific would prove to be one of the best calls during this wild and woolly season. The wildness was just beginning.

The day after the Pacific game, a blood clot was discovered in Tommie Frazier's leg. The sore calf muscle was not just a minor deal. This was a potentially dangerous situation.

I sensed a wave of great anxiety sweep across the state of Nebraska, as many fans expressed heartfelt concern. Television crews infiltrated Lincoln covering Tommie directly from the hospital where he was being treated. Tommie was put on anti-coagulant drugs to thin his blood. He returned to practice in non-contact drills during the week on the blood thinners with the hope of missing just one game. That would be the next game against Wyoming.

Enter Brook Berringer again. This time not as a mop-up player or even as a surprise substitution when Frazier would have to leave for an injury. Wyoming was going to be Brook Berringer's show.

Brook's life before and while at Nebraska portrays an interesting scenario. I had the opportunity to recruit Brook just after our 1990 season ended. That was the year we were recruiting some good quarterbacks: Clester Johnson, a highly rated quarterback from Bellevue, Nebraska; Tony Veland from Omaha Benson High School; and Kordell Stewart from New Orleans. They were all big, quick, and had strong arms. Brook was not as well known as the preceding three. Goodland is in the northwest corner of Kansas and it was a fairly snowy winter during that recruiting year. I kid Brook to this day that I never saw what the ground at Goodland looked like because it was always amass with snow.

Brook came to our football school while he was in high-school the summer prior to his senior year. He was an impressive looking person. At 6' 3", he had excellent size. And when you watched him throw with that smooth motion, he looked like an NFL quarterback. However, what was really impressive was his running ability. He could run straight ahead well, 4.5 to 4.6 seconds as a hand time in the 40-yard dash. Brook also had pretty decent agility. He had excellent character, kind of laid back—a hunter—also a great shot. During recruiting the following year, he shot some pheasant, and his mom, Jan, deep-fried it and fed some to me in shish kebab form. It was great!

Jan Berringer, an elementary school teacher in Goodland, was widowed years ago when Brook was very small. However, Mr. Berringer's twin brother, William, who is a pilot for Delta Airlines, resembles Brook in many ways. They are tall and handsome, but both have a reserve about them—a calm, quiet, thoughtful nature. William accompanied Brook on his recruiting trip. Brook wanted to be a pilot like Uncle William, and while Nebraska doesn't have a flight school, they looked for ways to enable Brook to get his pilot's license while he went to school and played football.

This outstanding athlete was not highly recruited considering his skills. Kind of lost in a sparsely populated area, it came down to Nebraska, Kansas, or Kansas State for his services. There were those who questioned why we took Brook Berringer. We already had Clester Johnson committed. Kordell Stewart was interested and Tony Veland was possible, but hadn't decided yet.

Coach Osborne always seemed to like Brook. They seemed to be similar types in many ways. Tom decided on Brook over Kordell Stewart because he knew so much more about Brook personally, even though Stewart was arguably America's most highly touted quarterback that year. If Veland wanted to come after Brook's commitment, that would be gravy. In hindsight, it was another good move by Tom Osborne. Well, that decision some three years prior was certainly about to be tested as we geared up for a new chapter of "Unfinished Business."

3

Second Quarter
The Domino Effect

*E*ach Thursday during the last two football seasons, a good friend, Curt Kuster, and I have met around noon for 15 to 30 minutes of prayer and fellowship. Curt is a pediatric dentist and also a professor at the University of Nebraska Dental School. He is arguably the nicest man I have ever met. He is thoughtful, humble, and consistent in his Christian walk. During those moments, I have really begun to appreciate the refreshment of prayer to the Lord with a fellow man, as we open up our lives in front of each other. We pray for specifics regarding our family members, our own personal lives, our jobs, even the football players.

Before the Wyoming game, I prayed with Curt about Brook Berringer. We prayed that God would give him confidence to do his best. If, as the Bible says, "The hairs of our head are numbered," then I am comfortable in praying about details in the game of football also. I do believe, however, that whatever the Lord decides to do, it will ultimately be geared for Brook to develop a close walk with Him. Consequently, my prayers also need to be directed to that end. We also prayed for Tommie Frazier's health situation and recovery.

We were ranked No. 2 in the Associated Press poll going into the Wyoming game and were expected to finish off Wyoming, no matter which quarterback played. The national media generally felt that without Tommie Frazier, however, our chances of winning the National Championship were dismal.

Even I started eye-balling the forest and looking past each tree. Man, did we run into a tree on October 1. In a tense affair, we saw ourselves down 14-0 at the end of the first quarter, then 21-7 with a little over two minutes to go in the first half. A combination of big plays by Wyoming on offense and Nebraska mistakes, largely in penalties, stuck our backs to the wall.

The ball was at our own 36-yard line, with two minutes and 12 seconds on the clock before halftime. If there ever was a time to execute the perfect two-minute drill, this was it. We practice our two-minute drill every Thursday. The idea is to move the ball without using timeouts. We have to rely on ball carriers and receivers to get out of bounds and stop the clock.

Our players must learn clock management as we communicate to each other. In fact, the communication must be excellent. Each offensive player must have a sense of urgency because of the limited time left in a half or game, yet poise must be at a premium. When a player panics in this situation, it can be costly. The quarterback is essential in the area of leadership and precision. Brook Berringer put on a highlight clinic of how a quarterback should conduct a two-minute drill. He completed seven straight passes for 59 yards. A couple were tough clutch catches across the middle by Abdul Muhammad who had a big day.

Tight end Mark Gilman, a junior from Kalispell, Montana, enjoyed a four-catch day. That was especially exciting for me because I had been waiting for Mark to gain confidence. Even though Mark was listed as our No. 3 tight end behind Matt Shaw and Eric Alford, he was a No. 1 in terms of playing time. He has great hands and good power. Confidence had been the missing ingredient. Eric Alford was forced to miss the Wyoming game due to injuries and discipline. Matt Shaw was an excellent blocker but limited as a pass receiver. With the score in Wyoming's favor a good percentage of the time, and Berringer playing instead of Frazier, we had to throw and catch effectively. Thankfully, Mark Gilman was up to the task.

Brook scampered into the end zone just before the half after his seventh consecutive completion. The touchdown turned out to be a "broken" play. Our receiver in motion went the wrong way and brought an extra Wyoming defender to the side that Brook rolled out to. The play was still blocked well enough that Brook had some daylight to the end zone, so he took off. Brook has excellent speed for a tall, rangy guy. He does tend to run high—kind of straight up and down with little body lean. He got into the end zone but that long torso of his took a vicious shot from that extra defender in the area. Brook bounced up and we bounced back into the game, still down 21-14 at halftime.

In the third quarter, Brook picked up where he left off. His confidence soaring, he took off on a 24-yard touchdown gallop just three minutes into the second half. Lawrence Phillips exploded on a 40-yard run for a touchdown and Brook did it again on a run from 11 yards. With eight minutes left in the third quarter, our offense erupted and launched us to a 35-21 lead. Not only was the score still uncomfortable going into the fourth quarter, but so was Brook Berringer's breathing. I noticed during a timeout when he came to the sideline to talk to Coach Osborne and his position coach, Turner Gill, that he was wheezing a little like one would from an asthma attack. There was a *squeaky wheel* sound at each breath. I remember looking at Turner with a frown as if to ask, "What in the world is that noise?"

Wyoming out-scored us in the fourth quarter by a point, but couldn't overcome our third quarter offensive flurry. It was a great effort on both sides of the ball by the Cowboys. From our view, without taking anything away from Wyoming's effort, we did not play well as a whole. Defensively, we gave up 32 points and a bundle of yards.

Offensively, we had our moments, but we were not consistent.

How good were we? Did we have what it took on defense to beat everybody on our schedule including the Bowl opponent? Offensively, even though Brook had a great game, could we handle it all without Tommie? Speaking of Tommie, when would he play again? Regarding Brook, what was that squeaky wheel sound anyway? We soon found out. For the second consecutive week, our quarterback was hospitalized after the game. I was at home that Saturday night watching the 10 o'clock news when I heard of Brook's plight. I immediately called the hospital to see if I could get in touch with him or a member of his family. Coaching football is strange sometimes. You would like to get close to every kid, but realistically the ones you get closest to are the ones that you personally recruit or coach. I felt a sense of responsibility to speak to Brook's mom, Jan, since I recruited him. I finally got in touch with Brook's girlfriend who told me he had suffered a collapsed lung. When I heard that, *I* nearly collapsed! What was up with our quarterbacks?

Brook spent the night in the hospital and the next day, Sunday, the coaching staff anxiously awaited the diagnosis. It was a partially collapsed left lung that did re-inflate, thankfully.

The coaching staff worked through Sunday night till about 10 p.m. which is normal. As we were adjourning our meeting and calling it a night, Clayton Carlin, one of our graduate assistant coaches, informed me there was a phone call for me in his office. I picked up the phone and Bob Knowles was on the line, except this was not the same Bob Knowles that I knew. There was an incredible panic in his voice, the kind that makes hair stand up and shivers run through your body. I heard tears and fear as Bob tried to explain what happened. I don't remember his exact words, but it had something to do with his wife, Maria, being terribly sick. I was finally able to make out something about Toxic Shock Syndrome and that Maria could die. Bob said he had to talk to me, in essence to pray for Maria. The fear in his voice jolted me not only to pray but to get to him immediately. I told him I would be at Bergen Mercy Hospital in an hour. I called Molvina to let her know. Bob had called her before he had reached me at the office. As usual, she was extremely understanding and even adamant that I go to Bob immediately.

I hustled down to my car. It seemed I had been in a hurry all of my coaching life. I jumped in the car but got out after I put the keys in the ignition to place something in the trunk. I hit the trunk opener as I got out of the car. From a combination of a force of habit and anxiety over Maria, I hit the power lock and slammed the door. Oh, oh. Exasperated, I ran back to my office, had to borrow a key to get in the door, and then called Campus Security to come unlock my car. They finally arrived and eventually got the door open. Finally, I was on my way to Omaha.

At the hospital, I eventually found Bob. Words couldn't describe the next 30 seconds. My relationship with Bob had always been one that was somewhat intellectual and analytical of something we both loved, football. All of a sudden, football was a foreign concept. As we embraced, I sensed the incredible emotion he must have been going through. Just a few months earlier he and Maria had to bury Michael. I was at the funeral and remembered it was the saddest I had ever seen Bob. At this moment, with everything hanging in the balance for Maria, it was fear that was the emotion.

Maria was just 33 years old, suffering from a dangerous episode of Toxic Shock Syndrome—not something you hear about every day. She had attended the Wyoming game with Bob the day before and admitted to not feeling well at the game while they drove back to Omaha but thought it might have been a touch of the flu.

The next day Maria was looking and feeling abnormally weak. Bob took her to the hospital that morning because she seemed to be getting worse. While at the hospital, Maria's temperature sky-rocketed to 106.8 degrees. The hospital staff went into a frenzy. Bob's first thought was of Michael, as the hospital personnel sprinted Maria down the hall to intensive care. He was scared to death. Maria's blood pressure was so low it was barely registering. Her heart rate was over 140 beats a minute, more than double her normal rate. Her temperature continued to rise to a boiling 107 degrees plus, and her body was shutting down. Bob's physician friend, Ed Taylor, quickly and correctly diagnosed Toxic Shock Syndrome. Dr. Taylor recommended aggressive treatment. Maria's condition was very critical.

For about 30 seconds, Bob and I embraced. As he shook in my arms, all of the emotions of Maria's diagnosis, the memory of Michael's death, his three other children, and what would happen if Maria didn't make it seeped through that embrace. I was surprised I was allowed to visit Maria. I was even more surprised she recognized me. She was glassy-eyed but conscious. She even had a peace about her the rest of us seemed to lack at that moment.

It all seemed to be out of control—family trying to be cheery but to no avail. There were long silences. As I saw what an emotional wreck Bob was, I couldn't take it anymore. I suggested it was time to pray. We walked down the silent hospital corridor looking for a quiet place where there was little risk of interruption. We finally found an unoccupied waiting room and began to pray to the Lord. There was depth to our prayers. We beseeched the Lord to save Maria, to bless Bob's other children as their mother's life hung in the balance during these crucial overnight hours, and for Bob to stand like a rock.

I remember vividly, as Bob prayed aloud, how unselfish his prayer was. He asked the Lord for His will to be done, that if He decided to take Maria that night, for him and his children to stand strong. Bob shared with me later that he wasn't used to praying out loud, but after he poured his heart out to God, he experienced more peace than he felt all night long.

The Apostle Paul, inspired by the Holy Spirit, wrote these words of encouragement in prison, "Rejoice in the Lord always and again I say rejoice. Let your moderation be known unto all men, the Lord is at hand. Be anxious for nothing but in everything by prayer and supplication with thanksgiving let your requests be made known unto God. And the peace of God which passes all understanding will keep your hearts and minds through Christ Jesus" (Philippians 4:4-7). Perhaps it was the peace of God which passes all understanding that Bob began to experience that fearful night of October 2.

After spending a little more time with Bob and his family, and with Maria still on a slow downward spiral, I decided to get a hotel room at the Holiday Inn. I have to admit I have an incredibly unselfish wife. Nearly four months pregnant and suffering the uncomfortable morning sickness common to pregnancy, she encouraged me to get some sleep at a hotel so I would not be exhausted the next day. I got to bed about 2:30 a.m. and was up about 5:30 to drive to Lincoln in time for a 7 a.m. staff meeting.

I called Bob before I left the hotel to see if there was any change in Maria's condition. The good news was that she made it through the night but she hadn't really improved and was still critical. I continued to pray. When I arrived for our staff meeting, I shared the story during the coaches' devotional. In our moment of silence, I prayed again that the Lord God of the Universe would have mercy and pour life into Maria Knowles. I presume the other coaches did the same.

Something like this could happen to any one of us. It doesn't always strike a chord inside until it hits home. What if it was my wife in this situation? Bob Knowles was experiencing it full force on the "home front." He would need friends through this. Once again, the season of "unfinished business" was put on hold in my heart, while a dear friend's life wavered.

Often in life you have to juggle many balls at once. As we resumed practice on Monday, I was hoping that Molvina's morning sickness would subside. I was also hoping I would have the right frame of mind to contribute properly to this week's game plan organization for our next opponent, Oklahoma State. Okie State is always tough to play from an offensive coach's standpoint because historically they have blitzed us relentlessly. That kind of defensive pressure must be prepared for whether it comes or not. The players and I needed great concentration. I admit, it was kind of hard to concentrate when Maria Knowles constantly rang in my mind. Not far behind in thoughts was Bob—very much distraught. I called the hospital a couple of times during the day to get an update. After the first 24 hours, the downward spiral of Maria's condition had at least stopped. There were no major setbacks.

By Tuesday afternoon, the doctors attending to Maria began to see some improvement, although she wasn't out of the woods yet. I began to hear the pain leave Bob's voice when we talked. Wednesday morning there was a cautious joy in his voice that put a big smile on my face. It appeared God was breathing life back into Maria Knowles.

By Thursday, Maria was out of intensive care and recovering smoothly. God truly was at work. I know many might say medical science, good doctors, and lady luck were on Maria's side. I certainly don't discount strides in medicine and skill of hospital personnel, particularly Dr. Taylor, but I don't believe in luck. I think Bob said it best: "I choose to believe that God listened to us when we prayed; that's the reason we had peace. God responded. God decided to act." I believe God wasn't caught by surprise with Maria's sudden illness and near death. I believe He did answer Bob's plea. God truly is great!

There was more bad news back at the ranch. Brook Berringer had been released from the hospital on Sunday after his lung reinflated, but Tommie Frazier was readmitted to Bryan Memorial Hospital on Tuesday, October 4, when the blood clot reformed. He had minor surgery to tie off the smaller clot and was put on a long-term blood thinning treatment. Chances were slim for Tommie's return this season. It was a devastating blow for this young man and our football team. This was more than Tommie Frazier out for the remainder of the season; this was his life. Blood clots can be fatal. His survival was of greatest importance, yet Tommie does more than just "survive"—he thrives. I saw this clearly as the season moved on.

With Frazier out and Berringer injured, the national media and others implied the Cornhuskers were "finished business." There were those who had their doubts. The polls reflected those doubts to a degree. We stayed No. 2 in the AP poll after the Wyoming game, but dropped from No. 1 to No. 2 in the Coaches' poll. With Oklahoma State in town to start off the Big Eight season, we had two objectives: win the game and protect Brook Berringer's ribs.

Brook would play, but he needed a heavy flack jacket for protection. The two were at crossed purposes from our perspective. Offensive football for us involved a pretty complete option attack. Option football means your quarterback better be ready to carry the ball and take some tough hits from defenders. This is particularly true when you have a great I-back like Lawrence Phillips and you're missing the nation's most dangerous running quarterback, Tommie Frazier.

Defensively, from Oklahoma State's point of view, it would be smart to make sure that when we ran the option that they didn't allow Berringer to pitch the ball to Phillips, but rather make him keep the ball himself. Brook is a fine runner but had a weak lung situation, so to the best of our abilities we didn't want him carrying the ball very much. Still, option football has been big and productive in our philosophy since the early 1980s. Thankfully, Brook is an outstanding passer. What we missed in option football with Tommie out, we made up in passing with Brook in. That would be our approach: to utilize a strong inside run game, minimal option attack, and a formidable passing game that would nicely blend play action and drop back passes.

Once again, early in the game we found ourselves behind 3-0. We went ahead on Phillip's 2-yard touchdown run and the strong leg of Darin Erstad, pounding a 48-yard field goal through the uprights to put us ahead 9-3.

In the first half, one of my wide receivers forgot to crack block on Oklahoma State's safety man on one of our few option runs. Brook, who was carrying the ball, took another excruciating blow to the rib cage area. There was a wince from our sidelines, as he got up slowly. Needless to say, I was not pleased with my wide receiver on that play. Brook once again had a nice throwing game and Abdul Muhammad had some pretty snags. We went in at halftime with the score still 9-3 in our favor and generally not feeling very comfortable about it.

Coach Osborne, as usual, systematically and calmly began to diagnose the diagrams of Oklahoma State's defenses that offensive line coach, Milt Tenopir, and graduate assistant, Mike Grant, had drawn up on the grease board. It was customary for both Milt and Mike to come from the press box before the half to have the drawings ready for Coach Osborne when he arrived.

The defense slipped off into other areas of the south stadium and the offense hovered around Tom and the rest of us offensive coaches. Tom just finished his analysis and his second half projections when a telephone was brought to him. It was a doctor on the other line. Our medical personnel had pre-scheduled X-rays for Brook during halftime and evidently the results were being forwarded to Tom. His expression while on the phone didn't reveal what was being said. Tom nodded matter-of-factly and politely hung up. With everyone listening as if E.F. Hutton were speaking, Tom stated that Brook would not be cleared to play in the second half. The lung was leaking again.

Immediately all eyes turned to our No. 3 quarterback, Matt Turman. I wish I'd had my camera. If there ever was a Kodak moment, this was it. Matt Turman, the boyish look-ing, unassuming walk-on from Neumann High School in Wahoo, Nebraska, a converted wide receiver, the son of his high school coach, broke out into an unforgettable smile. Instantly, the locker room exploded with cheers and several players rushed Matt to hug and encourage him. Who said college football is just big business? The scene in the locker room at that moment resembled a bunch of first grade kids getting ready to hit the playground for recess. Even though no one was happy over Brook's diagnosis, the players were convinced that Matt was the man for the moment.

The problem with coaches is that we sometimes over-ana-lyze. We look at statistics, goals, objectives, and logic, then try to figure it all out. After that, we worry. Matt Turman didn't have the running or passing ability of either Tommie or Brook. Matt does have excellent field savvy, but we were in a serious battle with the score only 9-3. Could it be done? If that halftime response had anything to do with the second half, then we had every reason to be optimistic.

As was customary, the assistant coaches left the locker room for the field before Tom and the team entered. As I stood on the sideline waiting for them, I noticed Turner Gill standing alone. I wondered what he was thinking regarding his quarterback situation. Turner and I have prayed together in the past over a variety of situations regarding our players and our personal lives as well. I asked him if he wanted to pray about this. Turner said, "Yes." Arm in arm, we handed the second half over to our Lord. We didn't pray to win, we just prayed that God would have His way. I believe that God does really care about who wins and loses. I even believe He decides the outcome. However, unlike humans, God doesn't define success by wins or losses, statistics, awards, or polls. I believe He seeks glory for Himself through those who want to serve Him. Such a one can honor Him in a win or loss, much popularity or none, a national title or a winless team. It's all how you play and whom you play for. All we could do now was to play and coach with the best effort for God in mind.

I'm not sure that it *was* our best effort, but the Turman-led Husker offense began to crank as our offensive line ripped through Oklahoma State's defensive front, and Lawrence Phillips was brilliant with a career high 221 yards on 31 carries.

Our defense, which had a sub-par performance the week before against Wyoming, was back to normal, limiting Okie State to just 136 total yards and 6 for 20 passes for 96 yards. Matt Turman looked like a poised vet as he handled our offense with precision. The third quarter proved to be big under Matt's leadership. We had two two-point conversions that day. One was great improvisation by Matt as he sensed pressure on a play action pass, flushed right, and hit Eric Alford on a pretty connection.

The second two-point conversion was also the result of improvising. One of my wingbacks, Jon Vedral, volunteered for the job that graduated David Seizys had done the past two years. Jon, like David—a scrappy, intense competitor—had the character to ask for the dirty jobs such as holding for extra points and field goals. It's a relatively thankless job, yet Jon Vedral isn't any fool. He knows the guy who does that job will probably make each travel game, especially if those "fussy" kickers and Kicking Coach Dan Young liked him.

The second two-point conversion was far from thankless. The snap was mishandled and Vedral had to chase it down with onrushing State players chasing him. It looked like one of the defenders draped around Jonny's legs would bring him down. However, Jon has good strength for a receiver and he stood his ground, desperately looking to pass the ball down field. That's exactly what he did, as an alert Darin Erstad, who just seconds prior had been ready to kick the extra point, ran for the end zone. Jon's pass looked like a casualty from duck hunting season but landed, nevertheless, perfectly in the outstretched arms of Erstad for the two points. It was the most dramatic play of a dramatic day in what was becoming a dramatic season.

The 32-3 victory was a special highlight for young Turman, as he accomplished what Brook had done two weeks prior, replacing the injured starting quarterback and leading us to victory. Oh, when the saints go marching in!

We remained No. 2 in the Coaches' poll but dropped to No. 3 in the AP. There was even more doubt among the national media as Brook Berringer was cleared to play again, but still in a vulnerable situation. We decided to play him only if necessary. Matt Turman, once again, was the man, but this time as the starter for the first time in his career.

Practice was interesting. With our quarterback injury status, we received national attention for taking a manager from our team, Adam Kucera, and making him a quarterback. Adam was a fine quarterback in high school. Nicknamed "Rudy" after the popular movie about a Notre Dame manager-turned-player, Adam received national publicity. Adam was a hard worker and although had limited ability as the quarterback, he served a great role on our scout team acting as the opponent's quarterback for our defense in practice.

Converted wide receiver Ryan Held and Adam actually played late in some games as quarterbacks when we had big leads, primarily to protect Turman and Berringer. Matt and

Brook would have to be prepared for a much improved Kansas State team—the best we had seen in years. It had been a long time, 25 years to be exact, since Kansas State had beaten Nebraska. K-State was undefeated with one of the top defensive teams in the country, statistically, and arguably had the most exciting pass offense in America led by All-American quarterback Chad May. May had ripped us a year ago in Lincoln for over 400 yards passing. K-State was ranked eleventh in the Coaches' poll and sixteenth in the AP.

ABC Television was on hand and this well-coached team led by Bill Snyder was sky high. There was a sellout crowd of nearly 43,000 in Manhattan. Only about 8,000 Nebraska ticket holders were allowed. For the first time in years, Kansas State had a legitimate home-field advantage. If ever the stage was set for a national upset, this was it.

Strategically, we expected K-State to play nine men on defense up on the line of scrimmage all day in order to dare Matt Turman to throw it deep. Two of those nine defenders would be their safeties. They knew we were limited throwing deep and running the option. Therefore, they prepared for an onslaught of inside power running.

To be honest, K-State has done a tremendous job in the last couple of years with an intelligent, aggressive 4-3 defense. But I'll guess Mother Teresa could have figured out that it would probably be three yards and a cloud of dust football from us. Just what the fans love, right?

The claim to fame in this game, however, was the Nebraska defense. There were critics who remembered what happened a year ago as Chad May and company had a field day. Not so in this one, as the Nebraska pass rush was too much for K-State to handle. We were ahead 7-0 after the first quarter and gave up a cheap touchdown on a broken coverage in the second quarter to make it 7-6. But outside linebacker Troy Dumas blocked the extra point. Dumas later intercepted May on a key drive and even returned it 54 yards. The

Blackshirts began to unravel May with a combination of six sacks and numerous quarterback hurries.

As the game wore on, just as May got rid of the ball, he took a pounding. Our outstanding cornerback, Barron Miles, was brilliant—breaking up six passes himself which broke the school record. Barron is a marvelous competitor who epitomized the word "dedication." Every day in practice throughout his career, this guy would treat every play like it was for the national title. He constantly challenged himself. I always rooted for Barron personally because when he excels I believe those great competitive qualities make a nice display case for the rest of our team to observe.

Offensively, as predicted, it wasn't pretty. My receivers had a difficult time getting to the K-State safeties to block them because they were so tight to the line of scrimmage, playing the inside run. Matt Turman really played admirably under the circumstances. He directed our offense well considering we only used about half of our repertoire.

Brook Berringer came into the game near the end of the first half just as we got within striking distance of K-State's end zone. We had two plays to stick it in. K-State's defense forced us into two fade patterns, one to Reggie Baul, the other to Abdul. Both were incomplete. Brook came into the game for good in the third quarter.

The key was to win the game and to keep Brook from getting reinjured. We didn't want him running the ball and if we threw it, he would need to get rid of the ball quickly. After a scoreless third period with a limited offense and a dominant defense, we finally struck gold in the fourth quarter when reserve fullback Jeff Makovicka began to rip through the K-State defense on traps and dives. His 15-yard scoring run put us up 14-6.

It was a frustrating day for my receivers. We knew going in we wouldn't throw much. With not much perimeter option running, even their blocking skills would seldom be used. They spent most of the day trying desperately to block the safeties that were sniffing around the line of scrimmage. They just couldn't get to them because of the safeties' apathy to our pass and perimeter game. The one bright spot came on a big fourth quarter, third-down play when Brook hit Abdul on a nice touch throw for 34 yards to preserve the victory. No question about it, it was the game of the year for us. We won. Our defense gained tremendous confidence and we got Brook through without further injury.

Even though it was a huge win for us, I reverted back to my receivers. They had really come along prior to this game. Abdul was getting back in the groove. The tight end trio of Shaw, Alford, and Gilman was playing very well. And Reggie, Brendan, and Clester were all having solid years. We had been catching the ball well and were having a great year of perimeter blocking. However, in this game Alford dropped a ball and it was tough to block. As Turner Gill and I drove back to Lincoln, a sports commentator on the radio struck a chord when he chastised my receivers for being too little. He was referring to the two jump ball-type fade patterns for incompletions that Brook threw to Reggie and Abdul before the half. Oh, it's nice to have big receivers, but our little ones have been very productive. It's hard to stomach criticism, though. I take it personally and want to defend my players, yet I know this defensive attitude is not a Christ-like characteristic. The Lord wants me to smile when the heat of challenge and accusation is turned up. He is in charge and nothing, criticism or praise, crosses His desk without His stamp of approval. I prayed that God would give me and my receivers the confidence to grow and improve the rest of the season.

It had been a few weeks since I felt sorry for my receivers and myself. I didn't miss the pity parties. It bothered me to start feeling this way again. I began noticing a guy who should have been conducting the biggest pity party of all—

the "forgotten" Tommie Frazier. He was declared out for the season and after the still-potentially dangerous news of the blood clot began to wear off in the minds of many, there was Tommie, coming to the meetings, watching films, encouraging the other players. What maturity! It's very hard for an injured player to keep showing up for our team meetings, practices, games, and gatherings. Even though he is welcome and generally encouraged by fellow players and coaches, he may wonder how he fits in. Most of the attention goes to the players who are active.

It does become easy to forget about the injured player. It's the injured player himself who senses this more than anyone. That's what I admired about Tommie. He was a preseason All-American candidate, a great star in the '94 season, and then his plans were dashed with a "fate beyond his control." With the hope that he could return and then acting on that hope by preparing himself even when the dream seemed so far away, Tommie stayed active mentally and physically.

With Tommie going through all of this, how could I feel sorry for myself or my receivers just because some radio announcer stated an opinion I didn't care to hear? Sometimes I need to grow up!

With Brook growing healthier, I knew the passing game would be resurrected again. We still needed to protect Brook by greatly reducing the number of options that we'd run. We certainly would run inside, but we also wanted to get the passing game back in gear. Brook had completed a high percentage of his passes against Pacific, Wyoming, and Oklahoma State.

I worked the receivers hard during practices, yet was sure to do everything I could to build their confidence. I was trying to be protective of them. The offensive line, running backs, and quarterbacks received much attention and deserved it.

Even as well as our receivers block on the perimeter, it just isn't exciting for the media to highlight. I do remember that Mike Gottfried, former coach and present color analyst for ESPN, made a big deal of our receivers' blocking during our TV game against Texas Tech. As a former coach, his knowledge and appreciation extends to the significance of perimeter blocking.

I somewhat understand why people do not notice receivers and their blocking. Most are trying to follow the ball; therefore, the guys with the ball get the glory. Our offensive line has been the most publicized offensive line in America because we run the ball well. This year we had some talented individuals up front that received an extraordinary amount of praise. Consequently, I was like a mother hen looking for something to build up my receivers and then protect them from the media. Perhaps I was protecting my own ego as well. When I am finally man enough to admit it, I can humbly pray to the Lord to remind me that the game of life is so much bigger than that. If I was going to live for Him, I needed to be bigger than that also.

The Missouri game became a breath of fresh air for the receivers and a big confidence booster. With our defense making clutch plays and Brook back in the swing of things on offense, it became a fun game for me, particularly in the second half.

Brook hit Mark Gilman for the first touchdown catch of his career. Mark was really having a very fine season. He was very steady. The tight end trio was delivering each week with Shaw dominating defensive ends around the conference and Alford with his electrifying speed and big-play ability.

Brendan Holbein caught his second touchdown of the year with a great touch throw from Brook. I was particularly pleased with this one because Brendan is primarily a tough blocking, possession receiving split end. Seeing him execute a nice release on the cornerback who tried to hold him up at the line of scrimmage and then receive a longer pass than what he is accustomed, would help give us more balance in the eyes of our future opponents.

In the fourth quarter, on a great play fake by Brook, Reggie Baul got behind the Missouri secondary for another deep touchdown pass. It was "bombs away," as Brook once again threw well and we had our 45-7 route going away. There was a negative, however. Matt Turman came in the game late in the fourth quarter to replace Brook and took a tough blow on his shoulder after a long run down our side-line. It didn't look good, as Matt was finally escorted back to our locker room before the end of the game with his arm hanging helplessly. I began to think of a possible shoulder separation and also what was probably on Coach Osborne's mind at the time—just what we need, another quarterback hurt. No time to worry though, it was time to trust God on this one, too.

Finally, what everyone was waiting for: the *Buffs* were comin' to Lincoln.

Following the loss to Florida State University, players and coaches from both teams joined on the field with a post-game prayer.

Prior to the start of the second half of the Oklahoma State game, Turner Gill and I pray for God's will to be done.

Former All-American Husker, Jeff Kinney, speaks at our chapel service, prior to the Orange Bowl.

Coach Osborne and company prepare to take the field against the Miami Hurricanes.

The early going wasn't easy, as Warren Sapp and his teammates make it tough for Clinton Childs to gain a few yards.

Reggie Baul prepares to run in a play from Coach Osborne. The receivers played one of their best games against Miami.

Sophomore I-back Lawrence Phillips runs for yardage against Miami. He rushed for 96 yards against their No. 1-rated defense.

Brook Berringer relieved starting quarterback Tommie Frazier in the first quarter. Later he fired a 19-yard touchdown to Gilman.

Linebacker Phil Ellis and his Blackshirt teammates harass Frank Costa during the fourth quarter.

Tommie Frazier returned in the fourth quarter to toss a two-point conversion to tight end Eric Alford and lead our comeback.

Molvina and her sister, Jonni-ann, share their thoughts on being pregnant. Both of them nearly gave birth the night of the Orange Bowl. Jonni-ann did give birth to, Duran Alexander Hughes, who I would later call "The National Title Baby."

A trip to the White House culminated a Husker harvest that included a National Championship and respect from everyone.

4

Third Quarter
The Campaign For No. 1

*T*hankfully, Matt Turman's shoulder wasn't a season-ending injury. It turned out to be a sprained, not separated, right shoulder that would keep him out for about three weeks. Here we were getting ready to play Colorado, who some felt was arguably America's best team, certainly one of the more physical, with just one experienced quarterback. In the end of the Missouri game after Matt's injury, instead of risking injury to Brook, we made a tough decision to pull true freshman quarterback Monte Christo out of redshirt. In addition, we were thinking of others on our team who played quarterback at some point in their high school or college career. Two of the candidates were cornerback Barron Miles and Clester Johnson. Barron was a great high school quarterback with excellent quickness, a strong arm and great intelligence and instincts. We decided to limit repetitions only to Clester, though, because he had played some quarterback as a freshman. As an offensive player, he had some knowledge of our numbering system, formations, and plays. The intention was to give Clester a few snaps per day, particularly when we were running options. As a coaching staff, we felt that Clester's strong suit was as a runner due to his great strength and durability.

Clester had really bounced back from that first game against West Virginia—which seemed ages ago. He was a valuable player. He did things you wouldn't notice, unless you were a coach or student of the game. The media seemed to like Clester. Maybe it was his great smile. He was quick to smile, easy going, cooperative, sensitive to others, and had a great team attitude.

During this week of intense pressure, media came from everywhere in America to profile the nationally televised contest. It was about that time that Clester dropped a bomb on me. Halfway through practice about mid-week, we had our usual daily regime of kicking. Clester and I had a little break in the action and sat together toward the side of the field. The bomb exploded when out of the clear blue, he informed me that when he was five years old living in Pasadena, California, he saw a man shoot and kill his mother right there in his home. Evidently, it was his mother's boyfriend. My heart nearly stopped in shock as I looked at Clester. The second emotion I felt was incredible remorse and sadness. I fought back the tears. I tried to converse with Clester in the brief interlude we had together and managed to sputter something like, "Do you think about it much?" Clester told me he tries not to think too much about it. Man, do you mean to tell me that beneath this warm, sensitive, coachable youngster with a great sincere smile lies this incredible tragedy?

A question has always challenged me. Are these players mere gladiators in shining armor that display their talents in front of multitudes on a Saturday afternoon? Stories like Clester's clearly remind me that these players in statue-like bodies are still kids in many respects. They have feelings, laughter, tears, emotions, anger, and friendliness, just like you and me. More importantly, they have a heart that contains a variety of experiences from the 17 to 22 years of their lives. Some of these experiences are beyond belief.

Those hearts need lots of love, but most important is that each one of these players has a soul. According to the Bible, that soul is going to end up in either heaven or hell. When I take the time to think of this, my perspective on our players changes. No longer is the final score the key issue. When I start thinking about their destiny, it makes the game seem small.

Perhaps I don't think about it as much as I should because the games often seem so big— especially this one. Colorado was ranked No. 2 and No. 3 in the polls, and just like us had one of the great offensive teams in the land. Some were comparing Colorado's 1994 triplets of quarterback Kordell Stewart, wide receiver Michael Westbrook, and eventual Heisman Trophy winner, running back Rashaan Salaam to Nebraska's 1983 triplets of quarterback Turner Gill, wide receiver Irving Fryar, and Heisman Trophy running back Mike Rozier. It was a legitimate comparison based on what Colorado had done to date. In a nationally televised contest against the University of Michigan in Ann Arbor, in front of the largest crowd ever to witness a college football game, Colorado made an amazing comeback that climaxed with an incredible Hail Mary touchdown pass from Stewart to Westbrook on the last play of the game for the win.

They beat a tough Wisconsin team in Boulder. They won a tight one over Texas in Austin while Salaam had over 300 yards rushing. He was also leading the nation in that category. Stewart was among the best in the nation's passing efficiency statistics as well as a dangerous runner on their speed option play.

Defensively, Colorado was tagged in preseason as the top defensive line in America. They have always been among the most punishing defensive teams in college football. I could feel the tension beginning to build during the week. It would be Nebraska's 200th consecutive sellout in Memorial Stadium. That truly is an amazing feat by our fans. I personally can't imagine a more loyal group of fans in the nation than what we have in Nebraska.

The excitement was building and what commonly happens when it does is overreaction. During the week of a so-called big game, players think coaches start over-coaching. Coaches start wondering if the players will respond to the challenge. I felt I worked the receivers as hard as usual during the week. And as usual, I challenged them with a written test on Friday. I gave them 35 to 40 scenarios they could experience during the course of the game. I threw some tricky questions in to stump them. I don't like giving out an easy 100% grade, but Matt Shaw was pretty consistent at 100% almost every week. Abdul was usually around 95%, but was always negotiating after the fact for that 100%.

After the very light Friday practice, the top 70 players eat at the training table and then go to a movie in town. After the movie, the players return to the Nebraska Center where they stay overnight before home games. Sandwiches, fruit, juice, and hot chocolate wait for them there. I normally take the receivers into a room where I give them their written test while they munch on their food. The test normally takes 20 minutes or so to complete, then they go to their rooms to finish eating, watch TV, and go to bed. Because the Colorado game had an earlier kick off time on Saturday due to national television accommodations, I decided to have the receivers take their test right after Friday's practice. I corrected the test while they were at the movie and then went over the test with them after the movie just before bed. These meetings usually are fun and provide comic relief from the intensity of the week. We all are usually laughing at Abdul sweet-talking me for a better grade.

The meeting before the CU game was different. Maybe I was tense, perhaps they were. I don't know, but everyone appeared to be uptight. They complained for the first time that the test was confusing—specifically the perimeter blocking phase of the test. Even Brendan Holbein, who does very well on the test and on the field in terms of assignment, said he was confused. It was a little late as far as I was concerned to be confused. Instead of quickly asking God for peace in this tense situation, I took it upon my own power. I lost my poise and began to raise my voice significantly. I believe raising my voice is needed at times, yet, in a controlled manner with God in charge. However, this outburst was on my own. It wasn't mean, ridiculing, or profane—just an act of disappointment, frustration, and fear. After firmly going over the perimeter blocking assignments once again on the grease board, I finally closed by telling them the assignments were easy and there shouldn't be any problems. I believe at that time the receivers were resigned to getting out of that room—pronto!

I went upstairs to my room at the Nebraska Center, flustered. This was the game of the year and my guys didn't seem to be ready. In my mind, even the trainers looked a little perturbed because I kept the kids in the meeting so long.

I collapsed on my bed in despair. I called on God and asked for His help. I asked Him to forgive me for trying to coach on my own power and leaving Him out of it. I seemed to have made a mess of things. I tried to do right and maybe that was the problem. Too much trying and not enough trusting. I knew it had bothered me. Tears were in my eyes. Where was this peace? I decided to call Brendan Holbein on the phone. Brendan's voice was pleasant, as if nothing was wrong. I questioned him again over the blocking, just for my own reassurance. He said he had it down, no problem. I then got his roommate on the phone, Eric Alford. He, too, said no problem. I put the phone down feeling a whole lot better. These kids bounce back a lot quicker than their coach.

As I finally shut the lights off for bed, I still had a little anxiety. Were the kids just saying it was all right when in reality they were unsure? What about the other receivers? I had only gotten reassurance from two of them. This was a game that would have huge implications in both the Big Eight and national scene. Would they be ready?

The next morning after chapel service we had our team breakfast as usual. I was curious as to the mood of my receivers. They sat off in a corner like they normally do. I tried to see in their eyes if there was any confusion. I couldn't tell. Let's face it, I was still trying and not trusting. After breakfast, I met with them one more time. They were more relaxed—again my heart gained more strength. What a roller coaster!

On the field during the pregame warmups, there was one more ride on that roller coaster. The receivers had a horrible pregame. We looked like we had hands like feet—particularly sure-handed Eric Alford. Eric was struggling, but didn't seem to be as affected by it as I was. While I was shaking my head in disbelief, I also began to realize it was out of my hands. God would decide this day. My only job was to allow Jesus to coach through me.

Our first play was one that involved Clester coming in motion before the ball was snapped and then hammering CU's nose guard. Clester came in and just bombed that poor defender. That was the way we wanted to play this one, with reckless abandon.

Eric relieved my fears with a big third-down catch on a tight end delay that got us a first down. Cory Schlesinger rambled 14 yards on that same drive and the stadium exploded as we went on top 7-0. With our defense shutting down all of Colorado's cylinders, kicker Tom Sieler booted a field goal in the second quarter making it 10-0.

With a great game plan, Coach Osborne skillfully performed surgery on Colorado's defense: the inside trap game to the fullback, outside perimeter running and a nice assortment of play action passes, particularly to the tight ends. Eric and Mark Gilman were having field days catching short passes over the middle as we marched down the field with strategic precision. Mark caught a nice ball from Brook on the sideline. Abdul got a shovel pass and made some pretty moves weaving his way deep into Colorado territory. Eric made a great diving catch on the 2-yard line. Was this the same guy that dropped everything in pregame warmups?

I-back Clinton Childs took it in for the score and we led at halftime 17-0. Our defense had held Kordell Stewart to 2 of 6 passing for an amazing 7 yards. Meanwhile, Brook had completed 9 of 12 for 100 yards in the first half.

Late in the third quarter, we called a pass off of a dive option fake. It was designed to get Eric deep. Sure enough, the Colorado defensive backfield was attracted for a second on the dive fake to Schlesinger. Around this time, I had to resort to our big "Husker Vision" screen because there was so much congestion on our sideline that I couldn't see the development of that play. The "Husker Vision" got it all as I watched Colorado's defensive backfield jump up toward the line of scrimmage and the speedy Alford zip by. Brook laid a soft one into his arms for an easy touchdown and a backbreaking 24-0 lead. When the game finally ended it was 24-7, Huskers. While it was a picture perfect day on offense, it was our defense that deserved the MVP Award. The Blackshirts held CU to 314 total yards and did not allow them to convert a single third or fourth down attempt in the game. Our linebacker coaches, Kevin Steele and Tony Samuel, had to be pleased with their players' discipline against Colorado's balanced attack.

It was pandemonium after the game. When the dust cleared, I met Molvina (now five months pregnant). We had been invited by a couple we knew well to celebrate their son's tenth birthday. When we arrived at their house, I saw their son, Shane, and his friends playing tackle football in the yard across the street. I decided that playing with the kids would be a great outlet to relax. I had the time of my life. As I played tackle football with these elementary school boys for the next two hours on a gorgeous Saturday afternoon, I had some incredible memories. I played football many Saturday afternoons with dreams like these kids. Here I was, an assistant coach at one of the great universities in America, living a childhood dream. More importantly, however, as I finally collapsed on the ground with the great smell of grass and dirt so fresh, I had unspeakable joy. The joy of knowing Jesus Christ as my Savior and Lord. The joy of indulging in the pleasure of sharing with these little boys how important character is, remembering how my Lord relieved me of my fears the night before and early this morning. God's peace had settled through me during the Colorado game. I was basking in the *Son* shine.

We moved to the No. 1 spot in the AP polls and many began to take us seriously as a legitimate national contender. There was no question that beating Colorado as convincingly as we did, while neutralizing Kordell Stewart and not allowing Salaam and Westbrook to go wild on us, was impressive.

Yet our next opponent, Kansas, was a team with superb talent, particularly on the defensive side of the ball. Their linebackers and safeties in particular were quick, hard-hitting players. I was looking forward to playing them. It meant I could spend time with a friend I had missed for a few months now, our former recruiting coordinator, Dave Gillespie. Dave wanted to coach on the field, so when an opening came at Kansas, Head Football Coach Glen Mason offered the job and Dave accepted. Molvina and Dave's wife, Anne, are great friends and it was sad for them when the Gillespies moved south to Lawrence. It was especially sad for me. Back in January of 1987 when Coach Osborne brought me up for an interview for the receivers job at the University of Nebraska, the same job that Gene Huey had just vacated to become assistant head coach and offensive coordinator at Wyoming, it was Dave Gillespie who showed me around. Many of my first impressions of Nebraska were based on Dave Gillespie. He is a genuine, caring, fair, compassionate man whom I grew to love as a dear friend. Needless to say, even on opposite sides of the ball I would enjoy his company.

I didn't think the week prior to the Kansas game was particularly outstanding in the area of practice performance. It seemed that we were flat and maybe a little cocky. I couldn't quite tell. The pregame warm-ups for my receivers weren't anything to write home about. We appeared sluggish, unenthusiastic, rather ho-hum. I'll admit, Kansas was a difficult team to figure. They had talent and at times looked like a team that could compete with any squad in America, yet at other times they looked beatable. I wasn't sure which Kansas team would show up. Neither was I sure of which Nebraska team would show up.

Fooled again. Before all of the fans had settled in we had intercepted Kansas quarterback Asheki Preston twice. After the first interception, Tom Sieler kicked a 35-yard field goal. The second interception set up an electrifying 51-yard touchdown pass from Brook to Reggie Baul. We felt that KU's hard hitting safeties would be creeping up around the line of scrimmage for the perimeter run game as K-State did. From the Missouri game on, we used play action passes to counter safety men that were too eager to support the run.

Brook made a nice play fake and Reggie ran a sweet route, caught the ball, and went the distance for six. The Blackshirts made life miserable for KU. The Jayhawks completed just 8 of 23 passes. We also shut down their running attack that had hurt us so badly the year before.

Punter Darin Erstad had a big day, averaging 49 yards per kick including a 68 yarder. It was great to see Reggie explode for a couple of reasons. One was that coupled with the Missouri game, defensive coordinators around the league had to start keeping their safeties "honest" because of the play fake deep pass threat. Secondly, Colorado claimed after the game that we were unable to throw the ball to the wide receivers. If you remember, the picking was fairly easy for us on play action passes to the tight ends. There wasn't much need to hit the wide receivers. The Kansas game reminded our critics, as the Missouri game should have, that Brook had the ability to throw to the wide receivers and the wide receivers had the ability to make plays.

In my opinion, the biggest play to a wide receiver came in the second quarter. If my recollection is correct, we had a third down and medium long situation and we wanted to throw. We called for our shot gun formation which meant four wide receivers in the game with our quarterback 7 yards behind the center. The play would require the wingback to be the primary receiver on a short crossing route. I've always liked Abdul to run this. We hit Abdul on this play the last couple of years on a number of occasions. I called for Abdul on the sideline, but he had a queasy look on his face and complained of a bad stomach. He had said earlier he may have eaten something that disagreed with him. Clester bolted into the game instead. Kansas blitzed us on this play and Brook had to get the ball to Clester quickly. Clester, not normally the go-to guy in the pass game, froze the defensive back covering him with a slight head fake and sprinted across the field. Brook drilled a perfect pass and hit Clester in full stride. Clester caught it and simply ran away from the defensive back for an exciting 64-yard touchdown play. As the crowd stood to roar for Clester's anticipated arrival in the north end zone, my heart leaped for joy. Yes, it was a touchdown pass for the Huskers. More importantly, it was a big play for a young man whom I had grown to love and appreciate dearly. This young man's great smile hides the doubts and pain of a dropped football that led to West Virginia's interception in the Kickoff Classic, and that same smile covers the tragic death of his mother. Man, was I happy for Clester.

Our 45-17 win over Kansas put us at the No. 1 spot in both the AP and Coaches' polls, yet none of the coaches were allowing for much of a celebration. We remembered just two years ago in 1992, after the two consecutive nationally televised drubbings over nationally ranked Colorado and Kansas. After climbing high in the polls, we then lost a shocker to Iowa State in Ames.

So here it was, two years later, two big consecutive victories over Colorado and Kansas, a high national ranking, and a possible humility problem. In 1992, we did not have a good practice week prior to the Iowa State game. Tommie Frazier, just a freshman then, was able to play but was very gimpy from an injury. Our top two tight ends, William Washington and Gerald Armstrong, were both out with injuries. Just before that nightmarish game in 1992, I overheard one of our star players complain that he wasn't feeling well and wondered if he should play. Usually in what would be perceived as a "big game," you would have to hog-tie a player to keep him from the field. The problem was just that—the media, the fans and our team did not consider the 1992 Iowa State game a "big game," hence, the upset of the season. Unranked Iowa State turned over highly ranked Nebraska 19-10 costing us any chance of winning the National Championship. We went on to win the Big Eight Championship that year, but the blemish was unforgettable.

It was even more tempting to take the 1994 Iowa State game lightly. Iowa State was winless and we were ranked as the best team in the land. However, Iowa State Head Football Coach Jim Walden had announced earlier that this was his final season. Therefore, the Nebraska game was his last home game. Emotions for the Cyclones would be at a peak.

I've often wondered if Jesus differentiated between situations while he walked the earth. In other words, were some people's situations like big games to Him and others just not as important? It just seems to me that Jesus was extremely intense, compassionate, merciful, loving, gentle, and fair in every situation with every person. He took seriously everyone He came in contact with: stalwarts of His day like Nicodemus, the unknown and despised lepers; different and even hated races, such as the Samaritan woman at the well, and those of great political renown as Pontius Pilate. There were situations like being up all night in prayer just before choosing the 12, to hanging on the cross in absolute physical pain and agony and still asking God the Father to forgive those who treated Him so brutally.

To this Jesus that I've decided to follow, every game was a big game. I suppose that is how I should view every game and practice. Players over the years have asked why am I so intense and enthusiastic at every practice. I'd like to take that as a compliment, but I must deflect the credit to where it belongs—Jesus. When I'm on the football field playing for the National Title in the Orange Bowl, on a hot summer afternoon during our high school football camp, at a Husker football practice, or playing winless Iowa State, something wells up inside of me. It's a passion, a joy that I don't try to muster up. I feel God's pleasure while I'm coaching. No matter how tired I am, I experience His power in me. I still need to grow to experience all that He has for me.

In a nutshell, the Iowa State game was big. It was the most important game of our season. I think the players and probably most of the coaches were tired of being reminded of the 1992 game. That was okay, we needed to be reminded that we can't just show up and expect Iowa State, or any team, to just roll over and die.

It appeared the reminders were successful right away in the game. We went on an 80-yard drive to open up the game culminating with Lawrence Phillips going in from the 1-yard line. We really felt that we could run the ball well as Iowa State was near the bottom nationally in rushing defense.

However, Iowa State was a much better team than they were rated. They were also playing on great emotion for Coach Walden's next-to-last game. They closed the gap to 7-6 on two Ty Stewart field goals in the second quarter. We needed something good to happen because we were beginning to lose some momentum. It did. Brook engineered another two-minute drill just before half. It took us over the midfield mark. With the ball on Iowa State's 38-yard line and one minute to go, Coach Osborne decided to call a play action deep ball. I thought that Reggie was going to run this pattern. Reggie had become proficient on these deep passing routes due to his great speed. Abdul, however, took the side that Reggie normally would have taken. Abdul may be a tad quicker than Reggie for a short distance, but I'm not sure he is as fast as Reggie in a deep ball situation. At that point, I wasn't going to take Abdul out of the game because even though deep down inside I thought Reg should be the guy, you can never underestimate a determined senior who badly wants to win the championship. I saw a gradual change in Abdul's attitude during the season, but the week of practice preparing for this game demonstrated his intensity.

Abdul lined up for the play and as the ball was snapped I could see Iowa State's defensive cornerback drop fairly deep. He wasn't fooled by the play fake from our quarterback. It was going to be tough to get the ball deep to Abdul. Brook let it fly anyhow. As the ball zoomed out there, Abdul accelerated. He caught up to the Iowa State defender also running hard for the ball. Neck in neck, the two ran as the ball appeared to be heading over both of their heads along the goal line area. All of a sudden, Adbul left his feet and fully extended for the ball. Abdul always goes after every ball. I've never seen him turn down an opportunity to lay out and try for a great catch. Sure enough, this was one of the greatest catches I've ever seen—a full layout, legs and arms locked out for maximum aerodynamics, amazing hang time, the ball on extended fingertips, then locked tightly to the elbows on impact. The officials thrust their arms straight up signaling, and in the words of radio broadcaster Kent Pavelka, "Touchdown, touchdown, touchdown, Abdul Muhammad!"

Ahead 14-6 at halftime, we were still not out of the woods. It seemed we were playing to keep from losing instead of playing to win. There is a big difference in the two. Fear is a stifling emotion that tightens your motor skills and reduces your thinking. It also skews your perspective.

I could see the receivers were restless and frustrated, particularly when Iowa State's talented young quarterback, Todd Doxzon, hit Calvin Branch out of the backfield for a clever 58-yard touchdown pass that tightened the score to 14-12.

We stalled and stumbled around on offense. Very late in the third quarter, it finally looked like we got something going when Brook hit Mark Gilman on a crossing pattern that Mark took up-field for a 48-yard pass play. But once again we got sloppy with a bad pitch that led to a 20-yard loss and stopped a drive.

Even the normally cool Matt Shaw was upset with the inconsistency of our offense. As a sophomore, Matt got his first big dose of playing time in that infamous 1992 loss because of injuries to William Washington and Gerald Armstrong. He knew what an upset smelled like and he sensed something bad in the air now.

I got all the receivers around me. They had made some big plays in this game, yet they were complaining about the score being so close. I reminded them of the good they had done and that the closeness of the score was another test of character. I admonished them regarding their character, which at that moment wasn't good. We had to grit it out and eventually the good things would begin to happen, and they did. Our defense was sensational again, other than the one big pass play. The Blackshirts shut down Iowa State's wishbone running attack that had hurt us badly in 1992. Iowa State's 62 yards on 43 carries are the kind of numbers you look for when defending against the wishbone.

Once again they shut down Iowa State's offense and Brook broke loose on a key run for 28 yards to ISU's 10-yard line. Damon Benning waltzed into the end zone on the next play making it 21-12, Huskers. It was a big sequence for us, but perhaps not as big as Doxzon's 32-yard touchdown pass to Jeff Turner that was called back due to a penalty. That, along with Brook's earlier scamper, may have been the turning point in a tough game for us.

Lawrence Phillips, who went over the 2,000-yard career rushing mark, scored in the fourth quarter and the 28-12 final score looked like an easier game for us than it actually was.

Were we flat? Not really. Were we sharp? Not really. Iowa State played with great emotion and vigor. How would the pollsters vote? Would we remain No. 1? To my surprise, we did remain in the No. 1 spot in both polls. I thought because of the struggle, since the scores were flashed across the national wires periodically and the score was 14-12 at the end of three quarters, that perhaps the pollsters would vote against us.

Some may think I'm out of line by saying so, but I truly believe the Lord had His special touch on our football team.

Something else took place that weekend that was even more surprising. Colorado Head Football Coach Bill McCartney announced he would retire at season's end. There were rumors flying everywhere of possible reasons. One was his heavy involvement as founder of the new Promise Keepers movement, a Christian men's ministry sweeping across America. The second was the health of his wife. Finally, the immense pressure on a notable head football coach in a top football program. I don't know why he resigned, but he may have felt God pull him in another direction. That was between God and Bill.

Bill McCartney takes much heat for his outspoken words. I will say this—I do admire the man's boldness and clarity. There is little doubt where Bill stands. In a day and age of many voices, many deceptive and unclear, it is refreshing to hear a loud Christian voice of clarity.

There was one more regular season game to go. The traditional post-Turkey Day classic, Nebraska vs. Oklahoma. It's always a great rivalry. In recent years, it hasn't had the same mutual impact for both teams regarding the Big Eight title and, consequently, the Orange Bowl. In fact, the Nebraska-

Oklahoma game has not had Big Eight championship implications for both teams since the 1988 game in Norman
where we beat them on a cold icy afternoon. That was Barry
Switzer's last regular season college game.

However, this 1994 game had historic meaning. A win
for us would mean an undefeated regular season with a 12-0
record. Only five teams in NCAA history had ever gone 12-0
in regular season play. Two of those teams were the 1971 and
1983 Nebraska teams.

More than this, for our 1994 Husker team, a win would
give us our fourth consecutive Big Eight championship and
our second straight shot for a national championship. It
wasn't going to be easy pickings. No question, Oklahoma was
having a tough season. The Sooners were 6-4 and head football coach Gary Gibbs had resigned, effective after their Bowl
game. Gary seemed like a nice man. I never had much contact with him personally. He was a great defensive coordinator for those powerful Sooner teams through the Switzer
years. Perhaps this year's Sooner team would be lit up to
make a great farewell for Gary.

Speaking of farewells, there would be four head coaching
vacancies in the Big Eight alone after the '94 season—Iowa
State, Colorado, Oklahoma and Oklahoma State. So you
want to be a coach, eh?

As was the norm for an Oklahoma game in Norman, we
had to travel on Thanksgiving Day. I personally love to stay
put on Thanksgiving Day. When I was a kid back in
Massachusetts, it often snowed and was very cold on the Day
of Thanks. My whole neighborhood, consisting of four
blocks of cousins, aunts, and uncles, would pile into
Grandma's house for all day feasting and football on TV. A
few of my older cousins would go hunting and bring back
some birds along with store-bought turkey, stuffing, potatoes,
greens, the works. Football and food, now that's what I call a
party! I miss those times.

Molvina went to San Diego during the holiday to be with her mom, dad and siblings. I felt lonely during the trip knowing there was our little child in her womb just a couple of months away from sunshine.

Thanksgiving night, after preparing the written test for the receivers, I watched West Virginia beat Syracuse on my hotel room TV. Man, had West Virginia improved. After a miserable start, they rebounded and won several games in a row. They were selected for a bowl game. I hoped the pollsters were looking at details such as this. It might have an effect how they ranked us after the Oklahoma game. Of course, it would all be a moot point if we lost to Oklahoma. Many had written off Tommie Frazier for the year as a moot point—except Tommie, that is.

I mentioned earlier that Tommie kept coming to team meetings. He would sit in on a number of quarterback sessions and watch practice. During the season, there just didn't seem to be much evidence, medically, that he would play, yet this guy just wouldn't give up. With the progress of the medication and several weeks without a blood clot recurrence, Tommie was finally given the okay to play. According to our medical consultant, there was about a 10 percent chance of a blood clot recurrence if Tommie played in the Oklahoma game. Our medical people left it up to Tommie and his mom. We decided to play Tommie only if we needed him, and he agreed. Brook was having a banner season. There wasn't a quarterback in the Big Eight that had a hotter hand. Brook was leading the league in passing efficiency and perhaps confidence. The confidence part is what intrigued me the most. When I recruited Brook a few years earlier, he had little confidence. I know most kids experience "nerves" just before entering college. However, I noticed even after Brook had been around a couple of years he seemed to be shy about taking the leadership expected of quarterbacks. Early in his career, I often pulled Brook over and encouraged him in this area. I thought he was loaded with talent, but he just wasn't sure about that talent. Neither I, Turner Gill, Tom Osborne, nor Knute Rockne for that matter can talk someone into being confident. Confidence usually comes from being prepared. Preparation is often a result of diligent training and learning though experience. Brook had finally gotten his shot this season and every game experience for him was a new learning lesson. Each week, he was becoming more prepared to be the field general we needed. His confidence was growing by leaps and bounds.

One day around mid-season when Brook was in the middle of his heated string of excellent performances, we had lunch together at the training table. Because I was close to his Uncle William, I decided to take the liberty to challenge Brook spiritually just a little. I was complimenting Brook on how he had grown more confident and the take-charge attitude he seemed to now display with ease. He was becoming a household name in athletic America, receiving fan mail from all over the nation. We laughed about his unassuming career at Goodland High School, the obscurity in the shadows of Tommie Frazier and then, BANG, a rags to riches story. It was then I decided to hit him with the Bible verse, Mark 10:31, "But many that are first shall be last and the last first." Now, I disapprove of taking scripture out of context, yet, I felt the principle that I was trying to get across to Brook was that God could take one from the depths to the heights and vice versa.

It is inspirational for me to see how situations can change so dramatically. It reminds me that anything can happen in football and life. Those in society who are feeling neglected and lost are noticed by God. He can change that situation in a heartbeat.

I didn't know what God was doing in Brook's life. My key objective was to remind him that God watches everything and that He desires to reveal Himself to this world even through the life of a tall, quiet quarterback from Goodland, Kansas.

Members of the Orange Bowl committee would be present for the Oklahoma game. Controversy had struck when the committee stated to Coach Osborne they couldn't guarantee our safety if we used the Orange Bowl's home locker room which happened to be the University of Miami's dressing room. If we beat Oklahoma, Miami was our probable opponent in the Orange Bowl game on January 1. The Big Eight Champ was officially the home team. We were entitled to the home team locker room which in most situations is larger and more comfortable. I'm sure the University of Miami was not excited about taking the visitor's locker room. I'm sure the Orange Bowl committee was not excited about telling the University of Miami they must take the visitor's locker room.

The story hit the media and served to stir commotion from the Miami police. The tag "locker gate" became famous in newspapers around the country. The Orange Bowl committee's position of not guaranteeing our safety was a personal affront to Miami security who had always done a fine job for our team. We decided to take the visitor's locker room, but perhaps the Orange Bowl committee learned a lesson from this.

Time for Oklahoma. It was a tough chore moving the ball against a vaunted and youthful Sooner defense. They had some defensive linemen who were strong and quick. In fact, we had minus 10 yards rushing on offense in the second quarter. We were going backwards!

It was 3-3 at halftime and our only salvage was that our defense once again was coming through. We knew going into the game OU's strength was their defense. Offensively, for the last three or four years they hadn't hung their hats on any particular philosophy. They did have a couple of fine running backs and some quick wide receivers. They had a freshman tight end that we recruited, named Stephen Alexander. I believe he will be one of the great tight ends in college football in the next couple of years.

It was tough going for our offensive line which was having a dominating year, certainly the most publicized year an offensive line ever had. We had trouble moving the ball on the ground and when we did pass we were uncharacteristically sacked three times in the first half.

As we came out for the second half, I happened to notice our center, Aaron Graham, wincing in pain. I've always liked Aaron. He is an intense young man who is articulate and business-like. He's an outdoorsman and I knew he had a good heart. I also knew that Aaron attended our pregame chapel services. Therefore, seeing him in physical pain and burdened, inspired me to remind him of the One that could lighten that burden. I went up to Aaron and whispered, "Hey Aaron, Jesus can get you through the second half." Aaron didn't say anything to me, he just painfully looked at me and nodded his head.

We fared much better offensively in the second half. After a very mediocre first half, Brook took off on a big 28-yard option run. On the next play he dropped back to pass out of our trips set where we line up Alford and two wide receivers on the same side of the field. We released Alford, Muhammad and Baul on streak patterns down the field.

Abdul was the primary receiver against the particular coverage that Oklahoma threw at us on this play. He executed a smooth release on one defender and then released straight down the field staying in his lane. Brook floated the ball between the underneath coverage Abdul had just eluded and the deep coverage that now converged on him. Just as the ball arrived, OU's right cornerback hit Abdul with a vicious whack. Little Abdul took a big-time fall but amazingly hung on to the football. Not only that, he was the first one to get up and demonstrate his toughness to 70,000 fans in the stadium and millions watching on national TV. The little guy with the gigantic heart was something else. That play set up Tom Sieler's 26-yard field goal putting us ahead 6-3.

On our next possession which extended into the fourth quarter, we put together our first and only touchdown of the game. On the first play of the fourth quarter, Brook dropped back and hit Abdul with a pretty pass after he made a nice one-on-one move on a deep corner route. The play covered 44 yards and finally set up Brook's 1-yard quarterback sneak that put us ahead 13-3 with a little more than 13 minutes left in the regular season.

Our defense held Oklahoma scoreless the rest of the game. It wasn't a pretty victory. It was tough and adverse. Maybe it would cost us in the polls, but we delivered the goods when we had to. Aaron Graham may have summed it up best, as he put his arm around me on the field heading to our dressing room. Amidst the crowded throng he exclaimed, "Jesus sure did get me through the second half, Coach." I agreed.

This regular season of "unfinished business" was not always pretty and smooth, but as far as I was concerned, Jesus got us through. He sure enough got me through.

5

Fourth Quarter
One More Orange Bowl Run

*T*he Nebraska-Oklahoma game wasn't the only key regular season finale. Auburn beat No. 3 ranked Alabama in their great rival game. Alabama was breathing down the backs of both Penn State and us in the polls, so the Auburn victory was a big one for us. Penn State put on a great offensive display against Michigan State. But MSU answered back with a fine offensive showing as well. Even though it was clear that Penn State was the better of the two, they had struggled on defense against the Spartans.

Our offense had a tough time against Oklahoma, but perhaps the pollsters were impressed with our defense and its domination since the Wyoming game. Comparing Penn State and Nebraska both offensively and defensively, it appeared that the Nittany Lions had the most prolific offense. Yet, we too had a strong offense capable of scoring a variety of ways.

Our defense was clearly considered the better of the two teams and that appeared to make the difference in the vote. At any rate, we were ranked No. 1 in both major polls and I wasn't going to argue with the verdict. As far as I was concerned, it would all come out in the wash anyway. We drew No. 3 Miami in Miami's Orange Bowl where they had been beaten just once in some 60 games. Penn State's opponent in the Rose Bowl was an inspired Oregon team, but most felt the Huskers had the toughest assignment. Winning the national championship for the Huskers would be like climbing Mt. Everest—possible, yet steep.

December is always a difficult month for our players and coaches. Our players start getting ready for final exams and we as a coaching staff hit the road to recruit. While this is taking place, we still have to figure out how to practice for the bowl game. We used to give the players about two weeks off after the Oklahoma game. The rationale was to let them study for finals, heal up after the long regular season, and let us recruit. But it's amazing how much a team and an individual player can lose physically, mentally, and emotionally with two weeks off. Offensively, with the precision necessary for an option game, we thought this procedure was unwise. We never seemed to get our timing back. Our players also seemed to lose interest and momentum.

Just after the 1993 season, Coach Osborne decided to practice the Monday following the Friday Oklahoma game in preparation for Florida State. The NCAA rule of seven coaches on the road at a time actually aided this practice philosophy. Three coaches had to stay in Lincoln and would conduct short but efficient practices every other day. This helped keep our timing and enabled the kids to heal and rest some because they were getting off every other day. It even served as a change of pace during their exam schedule. It's good for athletes and non-athletes to get some exercise during stress periods in life.

The other seven coaches could still do the all important recruiting necessary to have great teams every year. How can we measure this philosophy versus others? Many teams do it differently.

Prior to the '94 Orange Bowl, we lost six straight Bowl games. We were willing to try anything to turn that around. But the proof was still in the pudding. Even though we lost on the scoreboard, we had played very well on both sides of the ball—in some ways, outplaying Florida State. Our players played with precision, energy, and inspiration. Perhaps it had something to do with playing for the national title. But before paralysis from analysis sets in, we felt this practice philosophy worked. Therefore, we took the same approach for the '95 Orange Bowl against Miami.

Normally in years past, we would leave for the bowl site on Christmas morning and practice that afternoon at our destination. Before the '94 and '95 Orange Bowls, we left a couple of days before Christmas to get our feet on the ground a little earlier and get acclimated to weather and playing on the grass surface.

Playing on grass meant a slower game, particularly for a running football team. After playing on turf, it almost seems when you run on the grass that you are playing in deep sand. It seems like you use different muscles to get the same things done. We weren't unfamiliar with grass. Two days per week during the regular season, we would practice on our grass fields next to our baseball diamonds. It was a change of pace from the same everyday pounding on turf for our player's joints and muscles. As the weather gets colder, the grass fields get harder than the turf, so from November on we normally have all of our practices on turf. In addition, for the first time in many years, we played a regular season Big Eight game on grass. Oklahoma, before the season, decided to replace their synthetic turf with grass. It was advantageous for us to play on Oklahoma's grass field during our last regular season game. When we hit Miami, we were actually used to and comfortable playing on grass.

A trip to any bowl game can become terribly hectic. The players, the families of the married players, all of the coaches, personnel, administration, and their families all boarded the same plane to Miami. It almost seemed like the whole state was getting on the plane. It was great to see the children running around in the airport before we boarded. I looked over to my wife, Molvina, and touched her protruding belly. Our little one just about two months away from birth was kicking around in Molvina's womb, excited too, I guess.

We usually have a game-like scrimmage down at the bowl site to get us back in the groove of all-out football. "The scrimmage," would have the national spotlight on it. Tommie

Frazier had been cleared to play before the Oklahoma game. At that time, our medical consultants felt there was a 10 percent chance of recurrence of blood clots. The risk for the Orange Bowl was about five percent. Coach Osborne had publicly stated he would decide the starting quarterback after he and Turner Gill graded them on their practice performances and "the scrimmage" the day after we arrived. Practices were closed at our workout facility, yet the media would hang around and wait for the verdict. Who would be the starting quarterback? The defense really looked tough during the scrimmage. They were flying around making plays, having fun. Offensively for the most part, it was disastrous. We had the loud speakers on with the levels cranked up to simulate the noise in the Orange Bowl on game night. A number of players on offense were struggling to hear the quarterback's voice for cadence and audibility.

We went the wrong way a few times. To make matters worse, my receivers couldn't catch a cold in the Arctic Ocean. They dropped several easy catches. Tommie Frazier, despite the rest of the offense's ineptness, played well. You could see the return of his timing and his incredible competitive spirit.

Brook wasn't quite as sharp, but he wasn't bad either. The quarterbacks held up their end of the bargain. I was very discouraged. The receivers had really matured through the season and became consistent players who had the ability to make big plays. They had a tremendous perimeter blocking year and had only nine dropped balls during a 12-game season, which is extremely good. Seven of those drops came in the first five games. There were only two dropped passes in the second half of the season.

At Nebraska, I challenge the receiving corps to be under 10 dropped balls per year. It's a tough chore, but we've accomplished it six out of eight years. It takes tremendous concentration to consistently catch balls, particularly in the "frozen tundra" of the plains during late October and November.

So, what was our excuse in sunny Florida? We must have dropped seven or eight during the scrimmage. As I watched the receivers stretch after practice, I could see a little embarrassment on their part. Eric Alford, who had three drops himself, seemed to be in another world. Clester had a tough day. Every receiver except Abdul seemed to struggle. He played hard and well and was on a roll. I questioned my receivers and asked them as a group what was going on with them? Oh, I heard what I expected: Legs were tired from the trip, windy, not concentrating. Abdul spoke up and challenged us all, "We need to get it hooked up and get it going." Few words, but right on target.

The day after the scrimmage was Christmas Day. Coach Osborne gave everyone the entire day off. Molvina and I looked and called around to see if there were any Bible believing churches in the Miami Beach area. I decided to call Elsa Samuel, the mother of our outside linebacker coach, Tony Samuel. Elsa is one of the strongest Christians I have ever met. She is filled with love for Jesus. Every word from her mouth is filled with inspiration. I believe she takes literally Colossians 3:16, "Let the word of Christ dwell in you richly always teaching and admonishing one another in psalms and hymns and spiritual songs, singing with grace in your heart to the Lord." If anyone knew where a Bible believing church was, it was Elsa Samuel. Through the grapevine, Elsa heard of a church and its schedule for Christmas morning services. We had an address, but we couldn't find it. We drove and drove until it was 30 or 40 minutes past time for the service...no church. Pedestrians, residents, no one seemed to know where this "mystery" church was.

I wondered if this whole Miami experience was going to be a disaster. I thought about those crazy receivers again. How could those guys play so badly? Where in the world was this church? Where in the world was God?

I found out quickly where God was: in the back seat of our Orange Bowl courtesy car—smack dab in the heart of Elsa Samuel. She encouraged me to pull over into a parking spot. I submitted, ready to give up on everything. Elsa filled that car with song and praise to God. Molvina and I joined her in song. Since I was a little perturbed with the Lord, it took me awhile to mean the words.

Soon, I forgot my problems and began to think about Jesus, His birth, His plan for my life. Elsa began to read a favorite portion of Scripture, Psalm 65. As she read this Psalm, I sensed a calming inside me. I could see Molvina was ministered to as well. Verses 4, 5 and 7 really hit me the hardest, "Blessed is the man whom thou chooses and causes to approach unto Thee that he may dwell in Thy courts. We shall be satisfied with the goodness of Thy house even of Thy Holy Temple by terrible things in righteousness will thou answer us, oh God of our salvation who art the confidence of all the ends of the earth and of them that are far off upon the sea which stilleth the noises of the seas, the noise of their waves and the tumult of the people."

God chooses those who follow Him. He satisfies us with His goodness. He is my confidence no matter how bad or tough things get. God stills the earth's noise—all of those who talk trash, doubt our team, all those who think they have all the answers, who feel that they don't need God for everything. God is greater than all of the negative forces and influences in my life, even for those who doubt me, like myself at times. God could help me prepare my receivers to play the nation's top statistical defense. Man, did I need to be reminded of that.

Even though we couldn't find a church building that memorable Christmas morning in Miami, we found church anyhow...three Christians in a parked Orange Bowl car in downtown Miami Beach reading God's precious Word, the Bible.

I was so excited the next morning at our staff meeting that I read Psalm 65:4-7 to the coaching staff at our devotional. I began to thank God for His Word and how He blessed me with His peace.

Molvina and I had a wonderful time together. She had that glow pregnant women get. She looked beautiful and had a peaceful spirit. I was reminded of how much I loved and respected her. While I was at practice during the day, she would take the courtesy car and drive it around Miami, shopping, sight-seeing, you name it. Being pregnant and being alone never stopped Molvina. She has a fearlessness and determination about her. I've always admired those traits in her. She would sometimes hook-up with another coach's wife or a group of them for a specific function. In fact, all year long the coaches' wives as a group would get together for projects, charity work in the community, baby showers, etc. They are a compassionate group of women who do nice things for each other, the community, and certainly us coaches. For years, Tom's wife, Nancy Osborne has been a personal welcome wagon for assistant coaches' wives. When I was hired to coach here back in 1987, Nancy really made an effort to accommodate Molvina in the new environment. Since then, she and Molvina have done a number of things together and have a nice friendship. I believe each assistant coach's wife can attest to that. I've never forgotten Nancy's welcome mat nor her compassion for people at large.

Coaches Osborne and Gill decided on Tommie as the starter. Brook would play the second quarter. We would see how both did in the first half and make an on-the-spot decision at halftime to see who would finish the game. Of course, the media was waiting for the verdict and made a huge deal of it. The key was making sure both quarterbacks understood they would both play and each would have a significant impact in the game. Just as important was making sure our team would not divide over this decision. There were players in both camps, some favoring Tommie as the starter, some favoring Brook. It was a difficult decision. Coach Osborne had the final say and rightfully so. Everyone was expected to put aside personal feelings and be mature about it. The media can sometimes cloud up and intensify emotions, but our team had to be above outside forces. You can't blame anyone else for how you act. Each individual in our football program must be ready to unite on the same page, all for one cause.

I knew the Lord had a plan in all of this. He would have the final say in the game. Each man should be thinking, "How can I honor God with this game?"

I still seemed to be struggling with my own advice. I wasn't thinking about God's honor enough. As in that West Virginia game, I was dwelling on how badly the receivers played during the scrimmage. I was brooding, pouting, and wasn't thinking with the right perspective. I was thinking about my own honor, what little there was.

Practices were tough for my receivers. As a unit, their confidence was a little down, but they were trying. They pushed themselves. I drove them hard after practice working deep ball drills. I wanted them in great physical condition for the game. Graduate assistant Mike Grant, did a nice job giving the receivers a daily homework assignment that they would turn in at each morning meeting. At each receiver meeting, I would show them a Miami film. Three games were rather intriguing because they demonstrated that this Miami team, even though it was a great defensive unit, could be had. In my estimation, it was going to take three basic ingredients for my guys to even have a chance.

First, the University of Washington provided Miami's only loss of the season and broke their home winning streak. In that game film, you could see Washington's tremendous desire and physical conditioning. Washington did a tremendous job blocking Miami's defenders, which no other opponent effectively did all year. My receivers had to have the desire to block ferociously all night long—tight ends on their quick linebackers and wide receivers on their extremely aggressive safeties, particularly their All-American, C.J. Richardson.

Secondly, the University of Pittsburgh illustrated that Miami would let up emotionally and physically at different times. Pitt had a nice game plan and a fine running back and used both well. You could also see in this game and others that Miami was very vulnerable on short, intermediate passes over the middle of the field, particularly versus play fakes to the running backs. At times, their aggressive safeties would come flying so fast to the line of scrimmage they would be exposed to a deep ball.

Finally, the best film for my tight ends was the Georgia Southern game. Georgia Southern doesn't even use tight ends. They are a four wide receiver option team. But their offensive tackles had to seal Miami's outstanding sophomore middle linebacker, Ray Lewis, on their options. Georgia Southern doesn't have Miami's talent, but I noticed their offensive tackles working a hard step rip move technique. They really did the best job of any team of at least being in a position to block that speedy middle linebacker. I had our tight ends work that technique everyday during practice and encouraged them to watch it carefully on film. As usual, Shaw, Alford, and Gilman studied and worked diligently on this technique.

There were still too many dropped balls in practice. However, Abdul was not dropping the ball, he was catching everything in sight, working his tail off. Everybody else was working hard, but the confidence level still seemed down. We were just a few days away from the game.

On the receiving end of things, it appeared that Eric Alford was still not himself. He was catching better than during "the scrimmage," but he still wasn't reaching his potential. He had to improve. Eric had been a big factor all year as a dangerous deep and speed threat for us. Somehow, I had to get his confidence back.

It becomes very easy to over analyze as a coach in these bowl situations. So much was at stake. I could see the spiritual high from Christmas morning was wearing off. Psalm 65, as the rest of God's Word, has lasting power—it doesn't wear off. The problem is, I do. I allowed negative thinking about a dropped ball in practice, a missed assignment, or just watching Miami's great speed on defense to place my attention on my receivers' weaknesses, Miami's strengths, and my discouragement. Each day I had to go to the Lord praying, even tearfully for help. I studied the Bible anxiously looking for verses that would calm me.

One day during our coaching devotional, Tom Osborne read Isaiah 40:29-31, which assures us God renews our strength and provides the endurance necessary through adversity. That was the problem. I was soaking up God's Word and relying on some emotional high from that to get me through the day.

What I needed to focus on was not a feeling that would give me emotional energy to win the Orange Bowl game. I needed to yield this game to God and allow Him to retrain my thinking on winning in the game of life. What was my purpose in Miami anyway? What was God's goal for me rather than my own goal? How does God define success versus my definition of it?

These are questions that needed to be answered if my desire was to honor Him. I happened to bring to Miami a devotional workbook called *Experiencing God*. Coach Osborne, Lincoln attorney Fred Kauffman, and I challenged each other with some of the exercises in this book during our weekly Bible study. This workbook encouraged us to dig into the Bible regarding personal situations in our lives. When I had free time at night in my hotel suite, I reviewed the workbook lessons that had challenged me during the season. A concept from the author began to nail me again. God was doing a work... was I willing to join Him?

It seemed as though I had it all backwards. I was doing the work to try to win the Orange Bowl to maintain Coach Osborne's reputation, the Cornhuskers' reputation, my reputation. In the Gospel of John 3:30, it says, "He must increase and I must decrease." The Apostle John, in recording John the Baptist's statement, is saying in paraphrase to me, God is doing a work to exalt His Son Jesus Christ in those that trust Jesus as Savior and Lord.

Jesus must increase in this world, but also in my life. When people see me, do they see Christ living in me in my thoughts, words, and actions? Am I becoming more conformed to the image of Jesus Christ everyday?

As I challenged myself with this serious question, I couldn't say yes, particularly regarding the time I had spent in Miami preparing for this game. I wasn't decreasing in my estimation. Oh, my confidence wasn't high, I wasn't feeling particularly good about myself. I felt my reputation slipping among my peers. Although it appeared I was decreasing, I really wasn't. You see, I was relying on me. I was overly concerned of what others would think of me. I was the center of my life instead of Jesus Christ. It dawned on me that my only role in Miami was to let Jesus Christ live His life through me. God would determine what would happen to my reputation. All I had to do was coach as hard as I could for Him only, seek His applause only.

Excitement began to saturate me, as I felt the weight of the world fall off. I couldn't wait until meetings and practice the next day. I would join God in His work. I set my will to coach for God and enjoy the time. God would decide the outcome of the game, my receivers, my wife, that little child inside of her, my reputation. I could and would choose to trust this Orange Bowl experience and every other facet of my life to God, who is completely trustworthy.

I had a renewed confidence as the next day arrived. I saturated myself with 1 Corinthians 9:24-27, Philippians 3:13-14, and 2 Corinthians 12:9-12. I expected great things to happen. I believed that God would turn all of what I defined as weakness—poor scrimmage, low confidence, Miami's defensive ability—to strength. I began to see that with God empowering me I could not only hold up my end of the bargain, I could conquer any resistance.

As I worked the receivers hard after practice just four days before the game, they began to complain about how tired their legs were. I was interested in their feedback and listened carefully. But I sensed the Lord's peace inside of me and I spoke firmly to them, but with a smile. They would be ready to hit and run all night long against Miami. I didn't think they believed me, because the next day, just three days before the game, they complained again about how tired and sore their legs were—even tough Abdul, who was on an intense mission to win. While funning around later with a video camera, he admitted, "Coach Brown is killing me!"

Jacques Allen, who is our receiving corps' comedian, wasn't laughing a whole lot. He's got a great Scooby Doo cartoon character imitation, but even he was too tired to perform for us. I was confident their legs would revive. I knew we would do very little before the game now.

Former Husker tight end Johnny Mitchell, who now plays for the New York Jets, lives in south Florida during the off-season and came by the hotel to take Molvina and me to dinner. It was great to see him again—he's like a son to me. That's a great aspect of college coaching. You get to see young men mature. Even though Johnny's incredible talents allowed him to be a first-round draft pick after just two years of college, I was with him enough to call him "son."

Perhaps his greatest change was with his eating habits. He is a model for *GQ* magazine and others in the off-season, so he adheres to a low-fat menu now. Certainly a far cry from his college days when he would occasionally come over to our house and ask Molvina to cook him a whole pan of fried shrimp.

I was looking forward to being around the receivers in meetings and practices. They were still dropping too many passes as far as I was concerned. I couldn't tell how they would block because we backed way off on physical contact after "the scrimmage" to reduce any chance of injury. They were a little sluggish in their routes because their legs were still a little weary.

Even without many visible signs of encouragement, I sensed God's presence mightily inside of me. I knew I was on the right track. In the evening, I would hang out with Molvina but made sure we got to bed early. I wanted to be well-rested before the game. Before bed and immediately upon rising in the morning, I had my nose deep in my Bible, not searching for an Orange Bowl win, but rather a win for God. The fear was dissipating fast and was replaced with faith and great confidence. I kept praying for the proper perspective and to be filled with God's peace during this time.

Former Husker All-American and now Miami Dolphin wide receiver Irving Fryar spoke a challenging message to both teams at the Fellowship of Christian Athletes' Orange Bowl Prayer Breakfast. Also, Merritt Nelson, now an undergraduate coach working with me and the receivers, gave an excellent testimony on his faith in Christ to the thousands in attendance. The Orange Bowl Prayer Breakfast is the only event of a spiritual or religious nature that we make mandatory for our team. Each player gets to hear the gospel of Jesus Christ at least once during the year.

There wasn't much more to be done to prepare for the game. We wanted to make sure the New Year's Eve parties in the hotel didn't affect our players, and that our players didn't effect those parties either

I watched the NFL playoff games. I love watching football on TV with a frozen yogurt cone and a big bag of popcorn. I was able to get some frozen yogurt while in Miami. But man, did I miss my Nebraska popcorn. I ordered four big bags from Colby Ridge in Lincoln, and shipped them down to my Miami hotel, as I usually do on bowl trips. For some strange reason, the bags never made it to my room. I found out later Colby Ridge had shipped them out as scheduled, but someone else had signed for the bags. To this day, no one seems to know where that popcorn went. I do have a sneaky suspicion. There is another coach on our staff who loves popcorn almost as much as I do. I won't mention his name but his initials are T.G.! I have no actual proof, just a hunch. Ha Ha!

Our light day before practice at the Orange Bowl was full of energy. Evidently, my receivers' legs were well-rested now. They were running and laughing like a bunch of five-year-old kids on a jungle gym. We had to calm them down before they hurt somebody. I was at least pleased that their legs were back.

"The Big Day" finally arrived. The next order of business for me was to organize the pregame chapel for the Protestant service. Kenny Fischer, the former great Grand Island high school football coach, organizes the Catholic service and has always done a great job. This year, Coach Osborne put me in charge of making sure the Protestant service had a speaker each week. God has worked mightily in these chapel services.

Just about every Saturday morning the gospel has been preached with clarity by each speaker using his own God-given talents. This game wouldn't be any different in intent, but I had a few more people involved. The featured speaker would be Jeff Kinney. Gordon Thiessen, the Nebraska Central and Western representative for Fellowship of Christian Athletes, a publisher, and talented innovator in producing materials for Christian athletes and coaches, would introduce Jim Sanderson, a musician and singer who stayed up all night to write a song for our Husker team.

Jeff Kinney struck a chord with me big time. The former Husker All-American I-back and former NFL veteran gave an inspiring message from 2 Timothy 1:7 where it says, "For we have not been given a spirit of fear but of power, love and a sound mind."

Choosing speakers for the chapel service can be difficult. I want someone who is not intimidated by our players and coaches in attendance, namely Coach Osborne. We want one who knows the Bible and will preach it boldly and unashamedly, yet with a spirit of welcome, not condemnation. There are players and coaches in attendance who may not have trusted Christ as their personal Savior and Lord. We want them to know there is hope in Christ. Jesus met those who didn't know Him, right where they were.

Jeff was wonderful and my pastor friend from George, Iowa, Dan Hauge, who does a chapel every year for us, made the long trip down and closed up beautifully in prayer. It sure helps to have devoted Christian friends like Dan to keep me accountable in my walk as a Christian.

The day went on. I could feel the butterflies and sweaty palms. Coach Osborne and I happened to eat lunch together. Out of the clear blue, he said he couldn't understand how so many people all over this country were making this game life and death. That was a timely statement. As I was sitting in my hotel room before lunch, I had allowed my thoughts to return again to "what was at stake for me." Coach Osborne's comment reminded me once again that God needed my sole attention.

I took a nap after lunch because it was going to be a long evening. Win, lose, or draw, there would very little sleep for us this night. I also prayed and read my Bible to once again remind me where my focus should be during this game.

It was finally time to board the team bus and take the police-escorted trip to the Orange Bowl. The hotel parking lot, as well as the highway, was crowded. As we neared the Orange Bowl, we could see thousands of fans. Many were dressed in red and white screaming and cheering for us as the buses full of players and coaches passed by. Others were wearing green and orange and booing with thumbs down signs.

As we got to the stadium, the crowd was so thick that the buses couldn't get us very close to the locker room entrance. It was all somewhat humorous to me. As we got out of the bus people were screaming coaches' and players' names. They were mostly Nebraska fans encouraging us.

Then my eyes fell to a place that wasn't so humorous. There she was, so little among the masses, yet full of life—Maria Knowles. Bob was standing next to her. My heart stopped perhaps for a moment, as she smiled and shook my hand. It seemed that everything slowed down just for a second. This young woman, whose life was in the balance just three months earlier, was there to cheer us on. As I think about it, tears come to my eyes. I saw a living testimony of the tender mercy of God Almighty. Strength and a sense of purpose filled me up inside. I knew God was in control.

Normally, I just want to get right to the game. All the pregame hype bores me to no end. The Orange Bowl game has the longest pregame in football. After our pregame warm-ups, the team comes back into the locker room, but then we have to sit around for at least 30 more minutes. I always leave the locker room, go out into the stadium and watch the festivities for a minute. I then pull out my little New Testament from my back pocket and begin to read. I love reading Scripture in a full stadium.

I enjoyed the lights, but mostly I soaked up God's Word on our sideline, alone on the bench. I finally wandered back into the locker room as Coach Osborne was beginning to gather the team around. I had gone over the game plan in my mind the last few days. I had a feel as to how I should substitute the receivers. Speaking of those receivers, would they be ready tonight? Coach Osborne announced the kicking teams and personnel. And then, as was customary before every game, our whole team got down on their knees and we had a team moment of silence to pray. No one spoke. It was quiet. I prayed that God would be honored by our team, our receivers and me.

The game started a little discombobulated for me and the receivers. On the first play of the game, Brendan Holbein had an equipment problem. I assumed he was okay for the next play. Our formation called for two split ends and one wingback. Reggie went in at one split end, Abdul at wingback. Where was Brendan?

We broke out of the huddle and lined up with 10 men on the field. Brendan was still on the sideline getting his equipment fixed. We had to call a silly timeout already. I was mad, mostly at myself. I shook my head in disbelief, expecting a rebuke from Coach Osborne. My job is to make sure that the right personnel are in the game. I deserved a critique but never got one.

Coach Osborne called Tommie over to talk about the next play during our timeout. Coach Osborne never got flustered or upset. He must have known I would be hard enough on myself. I don't know. But I appreciated this man of compassion, in control.

Miami had tremendous speed and athleticism. They also had the gift of gab. There was some serious "woofing" going on out there. Before every game, Tom continually warns our players about trash talking, individual celebrations, and retaliations. What we're teaching our players in this regard goes against the grain of what they get with TV, movies, magazines, music, and the usual advice on what a "real man" should be. Our world says a real man should hit back when someone hits him out of line. A "real man" is a wimp if he doesn't get even. I believe that every theory and teaching should go through the grid of the Bible before it passes the validity test. When wronged, Jesus said, "Turn the other cheek." Many interpret this as weakness. But think about it for a minute. If I saw someone throw an unprovoked punch at another person, and the one who was hit, turned and said, "Go ahead, hit the other cheek," I would say, "Now that's a tough person."

Martin Luther King, Jr. took this principle literally and inspired the masses of victimized Blacks in the Jim Crow South to tough it out against their oppressors by turning the other cheek. This principle of non-violence helped the victim refuse to stoop to the same character-flawed attitude of the oppressor. I use this ugly reality of our past without the intention to offend anyone. This principle has been violated and embraced by those of all races. We live in a world of revenge. Hence, we, the United States, are the most violent nation on earth today.

These young men we coach from both teams are not immune from the vengeful, trash talking, violent world we now live in. The Bible says in Romans 12:19, "Do not take revenge, my friends, but leave room for God's wrath, for it is written: 'It is mine to avenge; I will repay,' says the Lord." A man who doesn't have self-control is actually a weak man.

We wanted our players to block, tackle, run and score with tremendous vigor but with their shoulder pads doing all of the talking, not their mouths or fists. This extremely important concept would perhaps play as big a role in this game as any one factor.

Miami scored first and was on top 3-0. We got a drive going pretty good, and then tried the same option action pass that Brook hooked up with Abdul on his great touchdown catch against Iowa State. However, Miami's talented defensive backfield played it perfectly, and safety Carlos Jones went up over Abdul to make an acrobatic interception on Miami's 3-

yard line. Even though the drive ended in disappointing fashion, there was a positive—our offense was hammering Miami's defense. Our tackles, tight ends, fullbacks, and Clester were getting to Miami's quick linebackers. You could see those defenders trying to overcompensate on their pursuit lanes to the ball carrier. In addition, the wide receivers were taking great angles on our inside runs and chopping down Miami's great safety tandem of Jones and Richardson.

As the game wore on, the impact that Brendan Holbein had on the blocking at the perimeter and then downfield was instrumental.

Slowly but surely, with one vicious blow to the legs after another, Miami's talented defensive backs began to wear away. It would not be a sprint mentality. It would be an endurance race, an all night affair. Nevertheless, Miami zipped an electrifying 97-yards in just five plays culminating with a 35-yard touchdown pass from quarterback Frank Costa to Trent Jones to make it 10-0 Miami at the end of the first quarter.

Our talented defensive backfield was a little tentative initially with the speedy Miami receivers. They gave lots of underneath room early. Miami was catching the ball in front of them and running nicely after the catch. Even though it seemed counter-productive, it was wise strategy by Defensive Backfield Coach George Darlington, to make sure our DB's respected Miami's speed early in the game, making sure no receiver ran by them on a deep ball. Hopefully, our pass rush would eventually wear Costa's body and nerves down. Costa was throwing well, but our defense stiffened in the second quarter. Eventually, our DB's would begin to diagnose Miami's passing game and neutralize it.

As planned, we inserted Brook in the game. On our second possession of the second quarter, we put together another nice drive. I had waited to use our speedy back-up wide receiver Riley Washington, on a reverse for several games.

Coach Osborne called a reverse and as planned, I inserted Riley. Brook faked a hand-off to our I-back and Riley came back in the other direction to take the ball from Brook. The exchange was good and Riley showed speed, agility, and second effort toughness on an exciting 9-yard run for a big first down. On that same play, Abdul came up with what I call a *stone,* a block that buckles the defender with force. That little guy is so strong and tough for a 160-pounder. The highlight of the play, however, was Riley's smile as he came to the sideline. It was probably in the same category as the Turman smile at halftime of the Oklahoma State game.

We now had the ball on Miami's 19-yard line going in. Coach Osborne called a bootleg pass in our two tight end formation. Mark Gilman was on the right side and Eric was on the left. Brook rolled right as Mark released well on one defender, collided with another, but had enough strength to stay on his feet and run toward the corner of the end zone.

Brook hit him with a soft pass for our first score: Miami 10, Nebraska 7. Both teams exchanged punts until halftime with us still down 10-7. I could see Miami was tiring considerably. They were breathing heavily. Our players were vigorous and enthusiastic at halftime. We were in great physical condition. All of the hard work, conditioning, and after-practice drills were paying subtle dividends. You couldn't see it on the scoreboard yet, but you could sense in the halftime locker room that our players believed they were getting the upper hand physically.

Miami superstar defensive lineman Warren Sapp, had played a tenacious first half, making several spectacular plays. He was one Miami player that didn't seem to tire, at least in the first half.

Coach Osborne, the receivers, and I talked about how Miami's two safeties began to creep up late in the first half to keep our wide receivers from blocking them. We warned them to tighten down their split from the tackle and tight ends so they could get a better angle to block them.

I reminded Brendan Holbein that he would most likely be in that situation much of the second half. I told him if he saw the weakside safety sneaking up that he should make a beeline angle to him. He should not start straight to the cornerback first, then crack the safety. If he did it that way, he would never make it to the safety on time. Brendan nodded in agreement. He had done his usual great job of perimeter blocking so far in this game. Reggie and Clester had also hustled and blocked hard in the first half.

Miami took the second half kick off and scored shortly thereafter, when speedy wide receiver Jonathan Harris caught a short pass and wiggled through our defense on a 45-yard touchdown catch and run.

Now we were down 17-7. Still there was a confidence on our sideline. Brook started the second half. Tom called a perimeter run to the split end side and I could see that safety man once again sneaking up toward the line of scrimmage. Brendan wisely tightened his split down as he was told. I licked my chops, this poor safety was going to get smacked. The ball was snapped, then lo and behold, the reliable Brendan did exactly what we told him *not* to do. He started straight toward the cornerback and then drove toward the safety, now running toward the line of scrimmage at the ball carrier. Too late! The safety exploded on a dead run into our ball carrier with Brendan just standing there shaking his head. We had to punt.

Coach Osborne and I went right to Brendan. Needless to say, Brendan didn't want to see either one of us. He took the "scenic" route to the sideline, away from us. I finally caught up to him and gathered all of the receivers together, as I usually do when our defense is on the field. This way I could talk to them all at once.

Now, other than this play, Brendan was having a great night, so I didn't feel like it would totally devastate him if I got after him a little. In addition, I was disappointed that he missed the assignment after it was explicitly explained to him at halftime. Brendan is a proud young man who is a great competitor. He wants to excel at all he does and I could tell he was a little embarrassed. I spoke firmly to him to let him and the other receivers know they must execute technique and assignment if we had any chance of winning. Brendan started saying, "Coach, I couldn't get there. I couldn't get there." That wasn't the response I wanted to hear. I sharply said, "You can get there. You must get there. If you are a champion, you will get there." Brendan didn't say much more but continued to shake his head.

Enter "Coach" Muhammad. All of a sudden, Abdul spoke up like I had never heard before. With firmness in his voice and an intensity in his eyes, he exclaimed, "We've got to stop making excuses. There is no room for excuses. Just get it done!"

Think about it. This same Abdul was the guy a few months earlier who didn't work out very hard in the summer because he was determined to redshirt and not play this year. This was the same Abdul who sulked after the Texas Tech game because his pass-catching string had come to an end. This same Abdul, because of that incident, frustrated and dejected, decided not to show up for practice the next day. Yes, this same Abdul, who began to focus and mature during the season, had become one of the great clutch players in college football by season's end. And now this same diminutive Abdul Muhammad, senior leader, stood tall in character and supported his coach's reprimand, and then reminded his teammates of his expectations for them—to play football, no excuses, get it done. I don't think I've ever been so proud of a player as we all put our hands together and on the count of three shouted, "Champs!"

This was a crucial time in the game. Our defense could have really "went in the tank" after giving up the early second half touchdown and then having to get back on the field shortly thereafter because our offense was sputtering around. However, Defensive Coordinator Charlie McBride, refused to let our defense feel sorry for themselves.

Miami had us on the run, but they seemed to lose poise and self-destruct with a couple of huge penalties that backed them up to their own 2-yard line. On second down, Husker rush-end Dwayne Harris, beat a Miami offensive tackle and accelerated to Costa who was dropping back to pass. Like a state trooper, Dwayne nailed Costa in the end zone for a 2-point safety. Now the score was 17-9 and Miami had to kick the ball back to us. There was still much time left in the third quarter.

After exchanging punts, we took over the ball again deep in our own territory. Brook was still in the game, Tommie on the sidelines. Again we put together another impressive drive. On this drive, Brook hit Abdul on critical passes for 16, 19, and 13 yards. A couple of those grabs were tough catches by Abdul.

We soaked up a lot of the clock and more importantly it gave our defense a good rest and kept Miami's tiring defense on the field. We were pounding away on every play. I paid close attention to the receivers' work ethic. No problem there. They were flying around like they were shot out of a cannon—chop-blocking the secondary on every play.

Tight end Shaw was working his tail off on Miami's rush-ends and linebackers. It was second and three at the Miami 31. We had put together our best drive, 72 yards so far. Then we made a mistake. Brook missed Clinton Childs on a hand-off as the ball and the drive bounced into the hands of a Miami linebacker.

Let me tell you, even though we seemed to be sticking ourselves in the foot, this was fun. Imagine playing in the National Championship game for the second year in a row after losing the first one. The odds were against us, as the entire nation watched. Even though I'm not a gambling man,

I'd bet that most of America was rooting for Tom Osborne and the Huskers.

Our defensive front four began to take control of the game. Frank Costa was taking hits after each pass. Once again, our defense forced Miami to punt, as the fourth quarter began. Miami was set to punt on their own 20 when the ball was snapped over the punter's head. The punter tried to kick it away from on-rushing Huskers. The official penalized Miami on the play after some apparent confusion for an illegal kick. It was first and goal on Miami's 4-yard line, our ball.

Coach Osborne called for a play action pass on first down where Brook would fake a hand-off inside and roll to the right looking for either of the two tight ends that released into the end zone. This was not a surprising play for Nebraska. We have been one of the best teams in the country at play action passes on running downs particularly in the red zone. We have scored numerous touchdowns in this same situation. No second guessing, it was a good call even before hindsight, especially against a physically tired defense just following a turnover.

As Brook rolled right, he had Gilman open early but it wasn't clear cut so he hung onto the ball. The crossing tight-end, Alford, was covered early, then came open. However, Brook was being chased hard and to throw across his body toward Alford against the quick Miami defense was inadvisable. He decided to throw the ball toward the sideline where we would settle for an incompletion and a second down. However, the pass wasn't thrown out-of-bounds far enough. Miami defensive back Earl Little, flew through the air like Superman and plucked the ball from the air, still getting a foot down inside the boundary for a spectacular interception.

In disbelief, our sideline exploded in emotional anguish. It was the only time during the entire game that I saw our sideline lose its poise. Even then, not all of the air came out of the balloon. Our defense held Miami once again. Coach Osborne brought Tommie Frazier back into the game. We went three downs and out but it appeared that Miami, on both sides of the ball, was exhausted.

We got the ball again, and Lawrence Phillips made a gallant 25-yard run for a first down to the Miami 15. Our offensive line and the tight ends were controlling the line of scrimmage. Sure enough, on the next play we handed the ball to fullback Cory Schlesinger who patiently found the opening and the way to the end zone. Abdul took that beeline angle to the Miami safety and kept him out of the play.

It was 17-15, and we went for the two-point conversion. Once again, we called a play action pass. Tommie rolled right and gunned a bullet through the middle of Miami's defense. I watched Eric Alford, the same Eric who had been struggling all week long with his catching confidence. Eric executed a quick release move on the outside linebacker and slashed across the middle into an open window in the Miami defense near the back of the end zone. I saw Tommie out of the corner of my eye yank that pass and I panicked for a second because Eric wasn't looking for the ball. The ball was streaking through the air, seemingly slicing up molecules and atoms along the way. Eric finally looked as the ball struck his hands and stuck like glue to tie the score at 17.

We were rolling emotionally. The momentum was clearly in our corner. As I rewarded the receivers with great down field blocking execution, victory was in their eyes. Once again we yelled one-two-three, "Champs!"

Our defense stuffed Miami again, holding them to one yard on the next possession and they were forced to punt to us. We took over on our own 42-yard line with about six minutes to go for "the drive." It took just seven plays. One was a diving catch by Reggie Baul. We had two crucial third down conversions. The first was on an option where Tommie showed his running expertise weaving and cutting his way across the field for 25 yards. The other was an option where tight end Matt Shaw drove Miami's rush end onto his back, opening up a hole for Tommie to squirt through for a 6-yard first down.

With the ball on Miami's 14-yard line, the crowd roaring, hearts thumping, and our offense licking its chops, smelling the goal line, Coach Osborne called a trap play for Schlesinger to carry again.

Big Warren Sapp exploded up the field toward Lawrence Phillips, who didn't have the ball. Matt Shaw dove at the linebacker and distracted him from the ball. Abdul took another nice angle to the Miami secondary and the cornerback showed up. Abdul drilled him in the thighs to knock him down, as Cory exploded into the end zone for the game winner.

Our sideline was much different than it was in the 1990 Colorado game when we went ahead 12-0 going into the fourth quarter; much different than a year ago in the '94 Orange Bowl with 1:16 left when Byron Bennett kicked a go-ahead field goal. This sideline was calm and confident. I looked up at Clester, as he kept shaking his head saying, "It's not over." Two minutes, 46 seconds left. This certainly was a championship maturity.

Our defensive backs were deep and our defensive line was laying its ears back to get Frank Costa as he dropped back to pass. Barron Miles and company knocked down a deep pass sandwiched by a couple of sacks which led to a fourth down desperation attempt. Kareem Moss intercepted that pass tipped by Tyrone Williams and it was sealed. Our offense ran out the clock.

I shook Coach Osborne's hand during the final countdown. I figured it would be the only chance I would get for a while. To be honest, I wanted to hug the man and carry him off the field myself. I'm sure there were many who felt the same way. Tom's faith, endurance, resilience in adversity, his compassion for his players and coaches weren't validated by the National Championship. He is all of that with or without a title. But the title would hopefully showcase that character America needs to see demonstrated by its citizens. Tom Osborne is a citizen to be admired.

6

Postseason
It is
Finished!

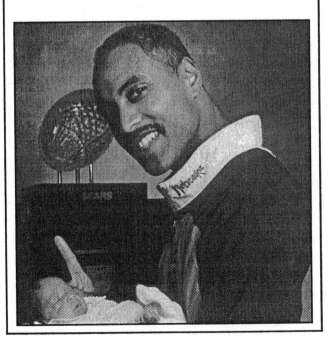

*O*ur sideline erupted as the final gun went off. After shaking hands with Coach Osborne, he was swallowed up in the mass of players, fans, cameras, and security guards.

Mark Gilman and I hugged one another and to my astonishment, he kissed me on the side of my face. His fuzzy beard wasn't very appealing, but the player-coach love of appreciation sure was. What a picture—a white, 21-year-old player from the mountains of Montana embracing a black 38-year-old coach from the East Coast. We don't see that snapshot in our society enough.

All of what the world defines as differences were overshadowed in that embrace of commonality of purpose and direction. When you are in a fox hole in the midst of war you are not concerned about the skin color, socio-economic status, or birthplace of the guy next to you. You are only interested if he's shooting in the same direction you are.

Mark Gilman, Coach Osborne, our team, fans, and the state of Nebraska had been at war a long time now. Tonight we had been in a fox hole in enemy territory. Few gave us a chance. Our backs were to the wall, it looked bleak. But we were all armed and shooting in the same direction. We had won the war not only on the scoreboard, but more importantly, we had won the war in character. Our players never gave up. There are many great starters but fewer great finishers. This was a great finish.

I noticed some Miami players draped across the battlefield, helmets off, some on their knees, shaking their heads.

I kept thinking about the Lord. The game was already a distant memory, a fog. I wanted to express to God my love and thanks to Him. Not just for the victory but the peace.

God had lifted me above my enemies of fear, doubt, and concern for my reputation during the game—those same enemies I had struggled with all week long. I was able to keep a cool, poised head, making good personnel decisions and suggestions to players and coaches.

God had wrought a victory in my heart. One thing was incomplete—that was to share my love and thanks because of my faith in Jesus Christ with others. When I saw those Miami players, I was struck with compassion and a desire to witness to them. I went over to talk to one of the Miami players. I don't recall my exact words, but as I touched his shoulder pads I said something to the effect that I understood how he felt. Prior to this game, I had been on the losing end of seven straight Bowl games. I also told him that whatever he thinks of himself right now, Jesus Christ loves him and has a plan for his life. I'm not sure it made much sense to him. He nodded his head. Perhaps a seed had been planted.

I headed toward the locker room when I decided to pray on the field before I left. I got down on my knees and thanked God for this opportunity. When I got up, a TV camera was sticking square in my face. I didn't recognize the camera man or his partner. I knew the interview had started because a bright light was on. He asked me what I was doing and I told him I was praying. He asked me what I was praying about. I told him I was thanking the Lord for this opportunity. You know, when the Lord brings you through a storm, you'd like everyone to know the excitement you feel.

When I finally got into the locker room, it was bedlam: noise, laughter, tears, and hugging. It was then, that Steve Pederson, our associate athletic director in charge of football operations, began to explain to me that Molvina had labor pains during the first half and had to leave the stadium with a police escort at halftime. I couldn't believe it. She was still a couple of months away from the due date. I tried to call her at our hotel room. The pay phone at the Orange Bowl wouldn't work. Steve's cellular phone kept fading in and out. I finally got through and then the phone line was busy. I had no choice but to wait for the team bus to depart for the hotel. I have to admit the National Championship didn't have the same glitter. My greatest concern was Molvina. Was she okay?

The team bus finally got to the hotel. It was about 2 a.m. I jumped off the bus and when I got out there was a pack of people near the hotel entrance. I spotted Tom Osborne quietly exiting the bus and heading for the side door of the hotel away from the crowd. Tom was so humble. He wasn't looking for cameras or praise.

I finally got to the hotel room. Molvina greeted me at the door and shared with me the story. It turned out to be false labor. She had called our obstetrician and everything appeared okay. She had some medication. Nancy Osborne, Tracy Peterson, Gayle Gill and former Husker receivers' coach Gene Huey, who had made a special trip to come to the game, had been very helpful to Molvina.

The phone rang a couple minutes later. Coach Osborne was on the line. He had heard about Molvina and wanted to be sure she was all right. Imagine that, it's 2:15 a.m. Coach Osborne had just won the national title. He could have hung around the adoring media and fans, but instead in his hotel room he called to check up on an assistant coach's wife. Well, that isn't too surprising, considering Tom's genuine character.

A few hours later, as dawn was arriving, Molvina found out that her sister, Jonni-ann, who was 9 months pregnant, went into labor while watching the game on TV from her home in San Diego. She delivered a baby boy. Yes sir, Uncle Ron would always remember, Duran Alexander Hughes, as the National Title Baby.

The next day was great. Thousands of fans from all over the state were waiting for us at the Lincoln airport. They were lined up across the snowy streets in two degree weather. The buses took the team to the Devaney Center where

15,000 fans had been waiting for hours in the basketball arena.

Tom and a few of our players spoke to the whole crowd. Cory Schlesinger received a thunderous ovation. The quiet fullback from the quiet rural town of Duncan, Nebraska, was not only their hero but America's.

Since that special moment, more wonderful things have happened to me personally. Molvina gave birth to our first child on February 18—a little girl whom we named Sojourner Elaine Carter Brown. Her middle name, Elaine Carter, is after Molvina's mom. Sojourner is dedicated to two great people in history. In the Bible, according to Hebrews 11:9, it says that a man named Abraham by faith "sojourned" in the land of promise. Our greatest desire for our daughter is for her by faith to trust Jesus Christ as her Savior and Lord, thereby making her a citizen of heaven and a sojourner—one who travels through here on earth. Sojourner Truth was a black woman in the 1800s who was born into slavery but eventually secured her freedom. She then risked her life to try and free other slaves. We desire Sojourner to have that kind of courage. The courage one day to trust Christ and secure her freedom from the slavery of sin. And then the courage to model Christ despite the risk and show others enslaved by sin what it means to be free in Christ.

Molvina's parents, Charles and Elaine Carter, came from San Diego to Lincoln just after Sojourner was born to help us "new parents" with adjustments. This kind gesture enabled Molvina and I to travel with our Husker football team on March 13 to Washington D. C. while Sojourner's grandparents watched her.

The White House trip, meeting President Clinton and other dignitaries in our nation's Capitol, were great treats for our team, as we were honored as National Champions. I especially enjoyed three Secret Service men who introduced themselves to me as fellow brothers in Christ. They were

Nebraska fans, but more importantly, we got to share some moments talking about the Lord. I also enjoyed the Washington Monument. As I looked across the expanse, I remembered what had taken place there 32 years earlier in 1963. I was just a six-year-old when Dr. Martin Luther King, Jr. gave his famous "I Have a Dream" speech.

My mind flashed to six years later when my dad and I watched the 1969 Texas vs. Arkansas game on TV, which turned out to be the National Championship game for that year. I noticed that everybody playing for both teams that day was white. I was 12-years-old then and very much understood where our nation was in terms of racism. I talked seriously to my dad about the issue from that day on. As I look at America since then, legal racial discrimination has been abolished per se. However, perhaps we must all admit that heart discrimination has not been conquered and snuffed out. That's what I love about college football though. I don't think it necessarily builds character. I do believe it reveals character. It brings youngsters from a variety of backgrounds and experiences together where much can be revealed about each as we strive together in a common quest. Winning the national title was a great honor—but the real learning for us came in the quest.

That's why I decided to write this book. The truth of the matter is simply that the National Championship doesn't have what it takes to solve any problem I've had since January 1. The trophy, ring, or even honor isn't going to answer life's real questions. It won't solve the race problem, the economy, or alcoholism. It won't keep babies from crying or dying, or thieves from stealing or murdering. Families are still breaking up and the HIV virus is running rampant. Most importantly, the national title won't fill the space inside our heart that is supposed to give us meaning, purpose, and direction in life. It won't reserve a home in heaven for us, nor will it keep us out of hell. It was never intended to.

For a moment in time, Nebraskans will have the pleasure of experiencing what it's like to be on top in the world of college football. However, that pleasure, although perhaps forever etched in our hearts, will eventually become dull and something else will have to come along to satisfy our craving for meaning. Then many will say, what's next?

In 1979, at the end of my senior year at Brown University, I finally came to the end of myself. I wasn't a national champion or All-American. Yet my small world still defined me as successful. I was adopted from an inner city orphanage as a little child by two wonderful people, Arthur and Pearl Brown, who became my parents. Neither, because of family responsibilities, finished their high school education, yet, with their inspiration, I was about to become an Ivy League graduate and sign a free agent contract with the Dallas Cowboys. Those in my world claimed I had overcome many obstacles to be this successful. Yet, deep down inside, the square pegs of academic, athletic, and social success weren't fitting in the round holes that could only be filled by the One who made me, God.

I had heard all my life about Jesus Christ. I believed intellectually and conceptually in Him, but I had no relationship with Him. I was living my life on my own, calling my own shots, making my own plans, pulling myself up the ladder of success by my own bootstraps until I came to an end of myself one day.

All of these things that I was chasing began to leave me high and dry with an emptiness inside. Some call it a weakness, a crutch. I thank God that I finally realized I was too weak to control life and make it revolve around Ron Brown. Every person, including myself, was too weak to totally fulfill me. I thank God for the "crutch" that He offered to me as a free gift—the cross of Jesus Christ.

Jesus as God in the flesh came down to earth, lived a sinless life, changed hearts, healed, performed miracles, was murdered on a cross for my sins, then was buried. That day in 1979, I finally realized only Jesus could give me the love, purpose, and direction on earth, as well as the home in heaven that I wanted so badly. It was then I banked my life by faith that Jesus rose out of that grave, back to heaven and is coming back one day to rule forever. That day I asked Jesus Christ into my heart. I decided to repent and turn from my sinful life. Jesus will enter and rule the life of anyone who believes and trusts in Him as Savior and Lord for forgiveness of their sins. That day was the greatest day of my life. It was the day I joined God's team.

I'm not always a great player for Him. I fail Him many times. But I am a team member for life and eternity. Jesus is my coach forever. Is He yours?

The best way I can paraphrase what I intended to get across in this book would be from a football analogy. Coaching receivers for the last eight years, I've come to the basic conclusion that even good players at times drop passes for three reasons:

First, the ball is coming and when it gets about six inches away from their hands they begin to think about turning upfield, juking defenders, crossing the goal line, becoming heroes. They then begin to look at the goal line just before the ball arrives. The ball hits their hands and drops to the ground. The first rule when catching the ball is that you must keep your eyes on the ball all the way in.

Second, when I'm drilling footballs at my receivers, I'm firmly admonishing them to watch the ball all the way into their hands. They nod in agreement, but their mind sometimes wanders. Perhaps they're thinking about the professor that gave them a bad grade, an argument with a girlfriend, or Coach Brown and "these stupid drills." Then the ball plops off their hands. They are seeing the ball, but the ball must be their only priority.

Then the third reason for dropping the pass is fear. In the 1988 UCLA game, our little 160-pound wingback, Dana Brinson, was reaching high for a pass. Just as the ball arrived, so did the UCLA defensive back with a devastating blow that knocked Dana on his back, hard. The first thought that came to my mind after he was pronounced okay was, will he ever come across the middle again to stretch out for a ball? So many times when a receiver gets hit like that, the next time he's wide open and the ball is coming to him, he will start to stretch for the ball, but then realize the last time he stretched out like this he got whacked pretty hard. All of a sudden those long arms God gave him to reach out and make great catches become like alligator arms. He begins to bend his elbows and not stretch out with great determination because of fear. Hence, the ball skims off of his hands.

The way I see it, God was like the quarterback in my life for the first 22-years. He had a ball in his hand in the form of His Son, Jesus Christ. For those 22 years, He kept throwing me passes. And for the same reasons receivers drop the ball, I was dropping God's ball, rejecting Christ. I had my eyes on this world and all the applause and the goals that people had set for me defining success, and I was rejecting Christ.

When I went to college, people encouraged me to go to church and join a Bible study. And every now and then out of a pang of guilt, I would show up maybe to gain a few points with God. But as I sat there I would get restless. My priority was not on Jesus Christ. I couldn't wait to get out. My mind would wander. I was rejecting Christ, dropping the ball.

Finally, there was fear. I was afraid of becoming a Christian. I was afraid of what my friends would think. I was afraid if I ever became sold out for Jesus Christ perhaps He would take fun things like football out of my life and make me a missionary in Iceland or something like that.

God gave me some "receiver coaches" along the way. They weren't the answer for me, but they were people that helped point me in the right direction. They helped me realize that there was something much greater than football, academic, or social success, something greater than success as the world would define it. Those things couldn't fulfill me. These "receiver coaches" helped point me in a direction so I could finally see the ball that God was throwing to me in the form of His Son Jesus Christ. I finally made the greatest catch of my life on that day in 1979.

As you opened this book, perhaps you were thinking you wanted to find out how the Huskers became Champions in 1994. But little did you know God was sending you on a pass pattern. And now the ball is coming at you. If you have never made that great catch in your life, the gospel of Jesus Christ has been explained in this book. Are you going to continue to drop the ball?

I tell the receivers at Nebraska, if you keep dropping the ball, guess what? We will stop throwing it to you. We will throw to someone else who will catch it.

You don't know when the final pass will come to you. None of us are promised tomorrow. I encourage you that if you have never trusted Jesus Christ as your Savior and Lord to reach out and make that great catch. Only He can make you a champion in life. Only He can fulfill your every dream and every need.

For those of you who have made that great catch, one of the other things I tell the receivers at Nebraska, after making the catch, is to run with the ball. Get another yard. Try to score on every play.

What happens so often after we've made that great catch, after we've trusted Christ as our Savior and Lord, is we limp to the sideline of life, beaten, worn down, afraid. We cry and say it's too hard to play in the Christian game of life. They tackle us for our faith. They call us names. They spit at us.

They persecute us. We sit down on the bench, head in the towel, crying, saying "I can't do it." And then Jesus Christ, the great coach on the sideline says, "Son, daughter, get back in the game. There are no bench warmers on my team. Everybody is a starting player. Everybody has a unique role in this game. And I've got a great plan for your life."

Some people are quarterbacks, in everything they do they receive glory. Some are offensive linemen. They get very little credit for what they do, but they open up holes for others to score. God has called each person in this world to a special role to make a tremendous contribution for Him, if they only give their lives to Him and allow Him to be their coach in every area of life. I encourage you to run with the ball. Go get another yard for God. When Cory Schlesinger dove into the end zone for the game-winning touchdown, the officials raised both arms straight up in the air. Every Husker player, coach, and fan also raised their arms in exultation! One day, God will be standing on the "goal line" signaling "Touchdown, Touchdown, Touchdown!" As each Christian *scores,* I can't wait to be in the "Heavenly End Zone" that day. I hope that you will join the team—*God's Team!*

Perhaps some, after reading this book, may question my approach to sharing my faith. Maybe, there are even those who are offended that I share my faith with others, possibly they're saying, "Your religion ought to be *personal.*" My only answer is this: First, I'm not involved in religion. I'm involved in a relationship with Jesus Christ, who I believe is the Lord God. Second, I believe my faith in Jesus is personal, but nowhere in the Bible does it teach that my faith should be *private.* The Bible teaches that we are to boldly take the message of our faith into every area of life. Psalm 119:46, declares, "I will speak of thy testimonies also before kings, and will not be ashamed."

Jesus' final words on the cross made all the difference in the game of life: "It is finished." The Husker football team finished its "Unfinished Business" in the game of football for 1994. Do you have "unfinished business" with God in the game of life? If so, Jesus Christ is ready to finish your business...forever!